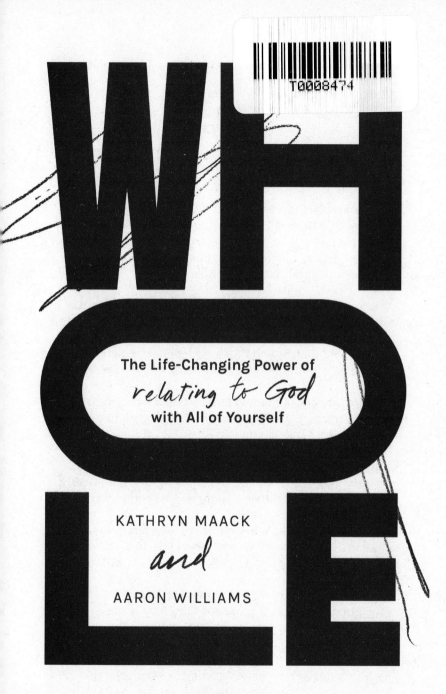

WHOLE

The Life-Changing Power of

relating to God

with All of Yourself

KATHRYN MAACK

and

AARON WILLIAMS

B&H
PUBLISHING
BRENTWOOD, TENNESSEE

978-1-0877-5562-5

Published by B&H Publishing Group
Brentwood, Tennessee

The authors are represented by Tom Dean, Literary Agent
with A Drop of Ink LLC, www.adropofink.pub.

Dewey Decimal Classification: 248.84
Subject Heading: CHRISTIAN LIFE / SPIRITUAL LIFE / TRUST IN GOD

Cover design and hand lettering by Matt Lehman.
Interior hand lettering by Kristi Smith, Juicebox Designs.

1 2 3 4 5 • 26 25 24 23

To BJ Maack and Mallory Williams: our faithful spouses
who have been a huge part of shaping this journey.

To our kids: we are praying with hope for your relationships
with Christ and the flourishing of the church in your generation.

acknowledgments

We are indebted to our literary agent Tom Dean, who believed in the vision of this book first, and to Daniel Cline for introducing us. Ashley Gorman—your editing goes far beyond having grammar skills and a way with words. Your big-picture thinking, theological accuracy, and knowledge of the broader Church have made this book infinitely better.

Finally, to some of the incredible thinkers and leaders that shaped us over time—your influence has helped us find our own voice. Many thanks to: Gerry Breshears, Michelle Bost, Aaron Keyes, and Jennie Allen.

contents

intro // half

Inhale.

Exhale.

Inhale.

Exhale.

Breathing. It is the act of moving air in and out of the lungs to facilitate an exchange in our bodies: a taking in of oxygen and a flushing out of carbon dioxide. Everyone agrees: breathing is essential to keeping our bodies alive and functioning.

Imagine if someone said this: *"But I'm just an inhaler. I don't do the exhaling part."* Imagine watching them *inhale* . . . and *inhale* . . . and *inhale*.

It wouldn't take long for that person's face to turn bright red and for both of you to realize that breathing isn't breathing unless you are inhaling *and* exhaling. When you think about it, choosing between the two would be an absurd choice to make.

Although we might not force ourselves to make this absurd choice when it comes to our breathing process, we can easily—and surprisingly—force ourselves to make it in a number of other areas of our lives. Especially when it comes to our personality or our spiritual lives.

In so many parts of our being, we tend to impose a dichotomy in the very place there should be wholeness. Where various parts of our being should be one, we rip them apart into two. For whatever reason, we've been blind to the fact that, like inhaling and exhaling, they were always intended to work together.

This book will discuss four of those interrelated dichotomies:

head + heart

spirit + truth

being + doing

saint + sinner

Do you separate these things? Do you put an *or* where there should be an *and*?

Without even realizing it, many of us have. We've segmented one aspect of who we are from the other, which, as we will see, has damaging effects on our overall well-being and almost always stunts our spiritual growth. Like a person who insists on just inhaling, many of us are unknowingly choosing to operate with half of the whole life God has given us.

If you feel far from God, or like something is missing in your spiritual life, or maybe you are just frustrated with the lack of real transformation that should be happening as you grow in the Lord, it could be that you are living out this sort of segmented spirituality. Maybe you are living as half of yourself and, therefore, are missing out on so much of the spiritual life you could be experiencing.

The four sections of this book, as we briefly mentioned above, give us a chance to explore the parts of who we are that we might be neglecting and offer practical ways to integrate those parts so that we can begin relating to God wholly.

Before you start, hear this: when you start relating to God with all of who you are, it is powerful. It is the way the Christian life is meant to be lived.

Do you want that? Do you want the pieces of you that are broken apart to be put back together? Do you want to bring every fiber of who you are into your relationship with God, including the parts you've been holding back? Do you want to stop relating to God with only half of yourself? Are you ready to come to Him with all of who you are?

Then get ready. It will change your life. Let's take this journey together.

section 1 : // head + heart

What was church like for you when you first started going?

In my mind (Kathryn) during my early growing-up years, church was like school, only a school where you dress up.

That's not really a criticism because elementary school was great. I liked my teachers for the most part, and I felt comfortable being in the building. It wasn't hard to figure out the system, you know, where you could do what it took to make good grades in the least amount of time. I could please the teachers and win the awards. I could figure things out for the test. Some information stayed with me ... the stuff that meant something for my life. I let the rest, the parts that seemed to have zero to do with my future, drop out of my brain as soon as the day was over. I liked school, but I waited excitedly every day for the bell to ring at 3:15 so my actual life could begin.

Church was similar. The smell of musty building mixed with old-lady hair spray (along with the occasional whiff of fried chicken—we remember you, Wednesday nights) was familiar. I liked the people. I could navigate the system and do well. I listened enough to the Bible stories to be able to answer the questions afterwards. I memorized the verses so I could get the next badge or certificate. Church was practically school, and I felt I was doing well at both: Scripture memory, the spelling bee, Bible stories, science lessons . . . they were all lumped in together. After many years of elementary school, I graduated with honors from both school and church. At least that's how I might have thought about it in my grade-school brain. I liked church like I liked school, but on Sundays I *really* liked when we got back in our station wagon to go home for lunch, when my actual life would actually begin.

— — — —

Eventually, I graduated from elementary school, and we moved to a bigger city and a megachurch that felt way more alive . . . current . . . smart. Long gone were the leaflets we used to take home with hand-drawn pictures of Jesus holding sheep. In their place were slick logos, advertising things that felt fresher and more forward. People seemed both intelligent and stylish at this church.

Apologetics and defending our faith against powerful messages in the secular world became the mark of a mature Christian. We could debate abortion and politics from a biblical perspective. We prepared ourselves to stick up for the Bible against anyone doubting its reliance. We studied things like *The Case for Christ* by Lee Strobel, who cross-examined a dozen PhD-level experts on old manuscripts, textual criticism, and biblical studies. We tried to memorize his solid answers to the tough questions. I was riveted by the evidence, and I remember idolizing those who could defend with articulate arguments the foundations of our faith.

I admired the people who made it all the way through the Bible. We started hearing more about people reading the Bible in a year. This faith journey wasn't for kids anymore; it was challenging. I wasn't wired to be a great debater, and I never made it through the whole Bible, but I was growing and excited to be a part of everything going on. I was stimulated by inspiring people of faith and talented leaders, and I watched with wide eyes.

The only problem was that I still placed church exclusively in the bucket of "learning about God," though now in more intellectually sophisticated ways. Held next to the stuff I was learning in high school classes—things like debate and history—it felt similar.

The problem was that I was still having trouble integrating what I did at church with my actual life. I was aching to close the gap between what I was learning and the real concerns of my heart: my parents' recent divorce, my issues with an unhealthy dating relationship, and more. So far, learning about God was helpful, but I hadn't seen Him pierce through to the real issues going on. Church was great, and looking back I know that my experiences there were certainly shaping me. But for the most part, it still seemed disconnected from the core of who I actually was.

head or heart

I do have a few memories in the musty church of my childhood that stand out as different from the rest. One was when the organ would begin to play hymn 150. Hymn 150 was "A Mighty Fortress," and even from the opening chords I was reminded of the power of our God on display through both music and lyrics. Without fail that song would start, and a single tear would fall down my cheek. I literally couldn't control it. I remember actually *feeling* something toward God. I would be overcome by the magnitude and power of His presence. It felt so out of place that I would always pretend my eyes were itching and secretly wipe that tear away.

You didn't do things like that when you were inhabiting the rows of the musty church. It was embarrassing to me if anyone asked, *"What's wrong?"* I didn't like to stand out, and tears in the middle of that environment didn't feel appropriate. Even more, I didn't even have words to explain them.

Over time I have realized that God wired me to cry when He touches my heart in worship. I can shut it down but only if I disengage from being wholly present to God in those moments. I did that for years, feeling it was more socially acceptable. It wasn't until much later that I began learning what it would mean to relate to God more fully. This journey with God couldn't just be an educational one but also a relational, experiential, and even emotional one. But somehow it was easier to blend in, to not be that vulnerable. It was easier to keep Christianity as something that only belonged in my head.

segments of myself

Unfortunately, I was more comfortable relating to God more as a distant figure to be understood than a person to be loved. As I reflect on those early years of my faith journey, I realize He was offering me so much more in my relationship with Him. He was inviting me into a depth of relationship that would engage every part of who I am.

As it is with any relationship, when we relate to God with only part of ourselves, we miss out on the depth of relationship He has wired us for. It takes more than our intellectual engagement to truly be transformed. While it's certainly true that we cannot know God without proper "head knowledge," as they say, the truth is that *education alone doesn't produce transformation*. God invites us into a relationship with Him that welcomes in our full humanity—head *and* heart. The more I realized this, the more I began to see snapshots of God relating intimately with people on the pages of Scripture.

Look below at these biblical examples of people relating to God in real relationship. Notice all the different postures outside of "sitting in a classroom" that show up.

> Adam and Eve **walked and talked** with God in the garden (Gen. 1–2).

Aaron, along with Moses, went from the presence of the assembly to the door of the tent of meeting, and they **fell on their faces**. And the glory of the Lord appeared to them (Num. 20:6).

Psalm 63:6 communicates to us that even in **lying down**, we can relate to God.

Psalm 98:4 reminds us that we can **shout** to the Lord.

In 1 Samuel 1:15, Hannah shows us we can **cry out** to the Lord in anguish.

In 2 Samuel 6:14, David shows us how to **dance** before the Lord.

Walking. Talking. Dancing. Lying down. Falling down. Crying in anguish. Shouting in praise.

It gives me chills to read these descriptions . . . seeing God so fully present to His people and His people so fully present to Him in mind, heart, and even body. God has given us dozens of examples of a whole relationship with Him. Nothing about the description of these relationships could possibly be contained by a book or a classroom.

When we consider these fully orbed examples of relating with God in Scripture, could it be possible that we have settled for less than what God is offering? Is it possible that we might not even realize the limitations we have put around the ways we relate to Him? Could it be that we aren't even aware that we have held parts of ourselves back?

What do you think? Do you think you relate to God with only certain parts of who you are?

For me, as I said, I had reduced my relationship to God to merely learning about Him. Maybe you are there, too. (Or maybe your experience is opposite of mine, and you hold your *mind* back instead—more on that in just a bit).

we all lean

If you find that your answer is yes to the questions above, take heart. The truth is, everybody leans one way or the other. For example, when it comes to the memory of your high school history class, some of you probably just loved learning about the Enlightenment, where everything was about the rational power of the mind. And yet others of you probably found that whole era too sterilized or cold and instead relished the unit on Romanticism, where the power of aesthetics and emotional feelings swept across the world's stage. You liked learning about one or the other because you, like everyone, lean.

Or in another example, consider personality types—we often designate mind-oriented people as "thinkers" and heart-oriented people as "feelers." Have you ever been labeled as one of those? Maybe you've labeled yourself, and like me, you're quick to lightly poke fun at those in the opposite category. Personality tests such as Myers-Briggs and many others will even confirm exactly which category we fall into and quantify what percentage of our personality is in each, further solidifying what "type" of person we are (or aren't).

Now hear me out, I am not against personality tests—I actually find them helpful in understanding myself and others. The point I am making is this: the categories of "thinker" and "feeler" become much less helpful, possibly even harmful, when we assume that because we lean one way that we don't need the other. If I'm not careful, I can assume because I am a "head person," I don't need to learn to relate to God with my emotions, or because I'm a "heart person," I don't need to read or study my Bible. Worse, I can begin to undervalue or demean the way other people, especially those different from me, relate to God.

This is why the greatest commandment God gives in Scripture is so helpful. It helps us know *how* God calls us to love Him. The great commandment says that we are to love the Lord our God with our **heart, mind, soul, and strength**.

All of ourselves. In other words, God doesn't let us off the hook based on the way we "lean." Rather, he calls us to the lifelong pursuit of learning to love Him with ALL of who we are.

For those of us feeling like we might be relating to God with only part of ourselves, the great commandment gives us a window into what it would look like to love Him holistically—with the *whole* of who we are.

A friend and counselor of ours, Jack, has spent the majority of his life and vocation working on dissecting this one verse. He drew us this graph to walk us through what loving God with heart, mind, soul, and strength looks like:

mind	heart
strength	soul

As you can imagine, when Jack helped us explore our walks with God, he explained that it seemed like we had been heavily loving God with our minds and maybe our strength. Although there are countless reasons *why* we lean that way, Jack pointed out that, as it stood, we sounded like we didn't know much about loving God with our hearts and souls.

I wonder where you naturally find yourself in this quadrant. I wonder what's easy for you and what's hard for you. For the thinker, you might like to read—that's easy. But maybe you have to challenge yourself to sing louder at church. Or maybe that Wednesday night Bible study comes naturally to you, but pouring out your heart to God in prayer seems strange or "too mushy." These things may be indicators that you may need to challenge yourself to love God more with your heart and soul. You may know right things about God, but you haven't let those true things bring you to a point of awe or worship in a long time.

For the feeler, perhaps you feel God's presence in conversation or in a song—this is natural for you. But on the flip side, perhaps you have to challenge yourself to study the Word consistently. Perhaps long sessions of prayer are a balm to your soul, but long sessions of book reading feel like torture. These things may be indicators that you need to inspire your mind in new ways about Jesus. You have a love for Him, but it's an uninformed love. You need to know more who the Word says He actually *is*.

I'll ask you again, are you more of a head person or a heart person?

Here are some general questions that might help you discover how you lean:

Are you more of a "head person?"	**Or a "heart person?"**
You love deep study.	You love conversation with friends.
You remember facts and details.	You remember experiences.

Are you more of a "head person?"	Or a "heart person?"
You think talking about feelings gets in the way.	You're sure talking about your feelings will solve the problem.
You value accurate information.	You value authenticity.
You own a lot of books.	You listen to a lot of songs.
You discuss theories.	You discuss personalities.
You go off on the facts.	You go off on intuition.

denominations lean

In addition to our personal leanings, we can also see how church denominations, organizational structures, and even corporate worship preferences play into the separation of mind and heart.

Odds are, you have chosen a particular church partially because it fits with your personality or leanings. You might have chosen a Bible church or more reformed tradition if you lean toward relating to God with your mind. You might have turned toward a charismatic church if you lean toward loving God most naturally with your heart. You might have chosen an Anglican church if you easily relate to God with your soul because of the depth of symbolism and liturgy in that tradition. Or a Baptist or Methodist church if you tend to relate to God with your strength, as they can tend to have more emphasis on missions or programs.

Many of us, before we were even able to choose denominations, were immersed in one that our parents or even grandparents chose for us. We might have been so immersed in that denomination that we never even realized its leanings within the church at large. For those of us who lacked exposure beyond our own churches, we might have either assumed our church represented the whole or potentially been suspicious of ones that leaned a little differently.

It's important to recognize both the strengths and the gaps in our heritage that has formed us. It can be insightful to know, not so that we can criticize but so that we can grow.

We can find security in the way our segment of the church tends to relate to God. We can consider our denominational leanings infallible if we don't have the humility to recognize that every denomination has gaps. We—every single one of us from every single type of camp—can walk in arrogance, assuming we have nothing to learn from our brothers and sisters.

Truth be told, if left unchecked, this tendency can even go beyond arrogance. Unfortunately, in the name of caring for the church, or theology, we can begin to spiritualize our leanings and demonize those whose leanings are different from our own. This creates unhealthy and unnecessary division amid denominations that would otherwise have the chance—if they'd only gather around what they had in common—to link arms in certain moments to do a lot of good in this world.

organizational segmentation

We not only see these "head versus heart" divides from a high level in church denominations, but we can also see them within micro leadership structures of many individual churches. In our most recent roles in our church, two of our main ministry teams were the discipleship team and the worship team. The divide between these teams was a strong one. Being on the discipleship team, I (Kathryn) was lumped in with what I would call "mind" people who viewed the worship team across the hall as "heart" people.

Our discipleship team loved to study. Most had been to seminary. They had common theological lingo and knew church history and terminology. They cared about the accuracy of the sermons and any teaching in the church. The walls on our end of the hallway were completely covered with books.

You didn't have to walk far for the sound of flipping pages to transform into the sound of guitar chords. Aaron's team, the worship team, had a totally different vibe compared to all our theology-speak. You could hear conversations about the way an environment felt in a room at the church. You might hear another about a personal situation in the church, and in response you would hear great intuition and empathy and calls for prayer.

Everyone on those different teams appreciated each other. But if you forced us in a room to talk things out, it would probably become pretty clear that we also looked at each other a bit dis-trustingly based on stereotypes—or rather, generalities—that spoke to our leanings.

The divide only became more entrenched as, in joint meetings, each team defended the rights for our own "side" without listen-ing to the other. The worship team would fight for presence and encounter. The discipleship team would ardently stand for theolog-ical accuracy.

The thing was, God was fighting for both.

If the Great Commandment is true, and it is, God wanted a fully informed mind and a deeply stirred heart at the same time, and I'm pretty sure He didn't care which team we were on or what our titles happened to be.

Part of the way He allows for us to learn the fullness of Him is to learn it from one another. That's hard to do if we're quick to consider others' leanings as less than or even heretical.

the divide in worship

Diving down one more layer, we can even find a divide within the realm of worship alone. Let's focus purely on church worship style for a minute, because the discussions over styles of worship are pervasive in almost every church. Sam Storms describes well the divide that can happen in his book, *Practicing the Power.*

Storms explains that people who tend toward loving God with their minds are most concerned with truth about Him being *accurately proclaimed* through the song. The focus of worship is to understand God and to represent Him faithfully in corporate declaration. According to Storms, for this group,

> **"Worship is thus primarily didactic and theological, and their greatest fear is emotionalism."**[1]

People who have a leaning toward loving God with their heart tend to focus on the emotional experience and the importance of personal encounter with God. Without downplaying understanding God, Storms says that these people believe that:

> **"God is truly honored when he is enjoyed. Worship is thus emotional and relational in nature, and their greatest fear is intellectualism."**[2]

In the end, we have greater fears of things "going too far" on the side that is contrary to our own leanings. When these fears of the people we see "across the divide" aren't given over to the Lord, they turn into divisive chatter, judgmentalism, and arrogance.

Our arrogance and infighting—even for something as important as worship—is fuel for the enemy's cause.

Our pride can also hurt the bride of Christ, His church.

an ancient problem

Did you know controversy between competing camps existed in biblical times as well?

Paul saw firsthand the divisions in the churches he visited, and he never neglected to remind fellow believers it was one of the greatest challenges the church would face. He reminded them to be staunchly committed to finding gospel unity among their differences.

When it comes to the Corinthian church, their differences were many. They were dividing over who had the best spiritual gifts. The rich and poor were divided at the Communion meal. Groups were dividing into various camps based on their favorite teacher. They were divided over how to handle meat that had been sacrificed to idols. They were even divided in lawsuits against each other. In almost every scenario, these believers leaned in all sorts of different directions. And yet, amid such countless differences, look at what Paul says to these Corinthians about their leanings:

> If the whole body were an eye, where would the hearing be? If the whole body were an ear, where would the sense of smell be? But as it is, God has arranged each one of the parts in the body just as he wanted. And if they were all the same part, where would the body be? As it is, **there are many parts, but one body**. The eye cannot say to the hand, "I don't need you!" Or again, the head can't say to the feet, "I don't need you!" . . .

> Instead, God has put the body together, giving greater
> honor to the less honorable, so that there would be no
> division in the body, but that the members would have
> the same concern for each other. (1 Cor. 12:17–21, 24b–25,
> emphasis added)

Paul spoke these words not just for the church in his time but as a reminder for us today. Between his time and ours, the church would divide more than forty thousand times, some over peaceful reasons and some for not-so-peaceful reasons. As much as Paul felt led to remind us to have strong doctrine, he never neglected to also challenge us to find gospel unity with those who held varying convictions in secondary matters.

Now, don't get me wrong—it's not like questions of theology or worship don't matter. They do. There are plenty of things we need to bring before the Lord and ask, "What's the best way to handle this?" The issue isn't whether we need to explore our differences or have hard conversations; that is not only part of walking with God but part of ministry too.

The issue is *who we are* in the midst of that stuff and *what we are really after* as we go about conversations about our differences. Paul is right to point us back to what—or rather, Who—we have in common:

> Now there are different gifts, but the **same Spirit**. There
> are different ministries, but the **same Lord**. And there
> are different activities, but the **same God** works all of
> them in each person. (1 Cor. 12:4–6, emphasis added)

I don't know which way you lean, which way your denomination leans, or which way your organization leans, but if you've expressed faith in the good news of the gospel, we have Christ in common. We have the Spirit of God in common. We have the same heavenly

Father in common. And we are members of one another, all part of the same body.

Pausing to remember this is not a way to dodge whatever question is at hand; it's to change our posture so that we might enter back into that important conversation with the right attitude toward God and our neighbor. It's to ensure that when we approach differences on secondary matters, we do so in love . . . and with a commitment to remain united on primary things.

What does all this mean? That not only do you need every part of yourself coming to God as a whole individual, but the Christian church in all places and ages needs every part coming together so that we might serve God with the whole, not leaving any part out.

But sometimes we choose to settle for less.

something's missing

The Barna Group surveyed a large segment of Americans who have attended church and reported these facts about their experiences:

- One-third of the people have never felt God's presence while in a congregational setting.[3]

The Barna Group also asked participants if their lives had been changed by attending church. Here are the responses:

- Twenty-six percent said their lives had been *greatly changed* by attending church.
- Twenty-five percent described it as "somewhat" influential.
- Forty-six percent said their lives had not changed at all as a result of churchgoing.[4]

Did you catch that? Most of the churchgoers sitting in the pews every week say they aren't being transformed in any major way as they participate in church. Now, who knows what people think *changed* means. Some might think *changed* means all their problems go away the minute they walk out the door. Others might think this means the church is responsible for giving them an otherworldly emotional high for the rest of the week after they leave. Still others might think this means God will give them everything they've dreamed of because they "paid their dues" and sat through service after service. And we all know that experiencing good weekly teaching over the course of a lifetime most certainly shapes a person over the long haul, whether they feel it in the moment or not. But still, that being said, *46 percent*? Even if we account for some subpar definitions of *changed*, that's a staggering number of churchgoers who say their lives aren't really being transformed.

As we said before, it's not just individual people who have leanings; it's *entities*. Could it be possible that this lack of transformation among churchgoers is linked to some of the gaps their church has in the ways it relates to God corporately? Could it be possible that a congregation full of "head types" aren't seeing life-change because, for all the Word of God they know and study, they've never experienced the heart of God? Could it be possible that a congregation full of "heart types" have the opposite problem, leaving them with a sincere faith but a woefully uninformed one?

When we relate to God with all of ourselves, He brings fullness of life to us individually. He brings fullness of life to His church.

But sometimes, for many of us, that feels too extreme. We feel safer when church is in a box. We feel like we can control our Christian experience by bringing only the part of us that we understand or enjoy.

fear of extremes

On a corporate level, one of the reasons we fail to relate to God holistically is our fear of extremes. We build distrust for certain growth pathways that aren't comfortable parts of our tradition. We even build stereotypes of other streams that help us feel good about the places we have planted theological stakes in our own tradition.

The "heart camp" criticizes the "head camp" for being void of feeling for the sake of getting the facts right.

Fundamentally, as we've mentioned before, the heart camp's greatest fear is intellectualism, and the greatest concern is that the head camp will reduce Christianity to an academic pursuit instead of an actual relationship with God.

There is a genuine concern that Christianity will lose its power and will turn into a stale religion or that relational closeness with God will be replaced by facts about Him. Words like *exegesis, Sunday school,* or *sermons* will often generate a less-than-excited grumble from the heart camp. And so the mark of success in these environments is not if God is actually worshipped or known for who He is but if one's feelings go through ecstatic highs and lows. Worse than that, sometimes those in this camp can worship *the experience of worship itself* instead of the living God.

On the other hand, the "head camp" criticizes the "heart camp" for the tendency to live from one emotional high to another. Some heart people have a way of expressing their experience or interaction with God that can be off-putting for the people in the "head camp."

Fundamentally, as we mentioned before, the head camp's greatest fear is emotionalism, and the greatest concern is that the heart camp will stray from biblical truth.

There is a concern that truth will be watered down by feelings. This is a legitimate concern. Words like *experience, encounter,* or *presence* are often seen as dangerous and concerning. Someone said to me recently, "These young people expressing themselves with so much emotion in worship is dangerous. They are just going from one emotional high to another. It can't be real." This camp often has a strong opinion that emotion can't be trusted and that the truest form of faith is devoid of emotion because emotion isn't *needed* in mature spirituality. And so the mark of success in these environments is not if God is actually worshipped but if right information about Him is rightly transmitted. Worse than that, sometimes those in this camp can worship a good learning environment more than they worship the living God.

I (Aaron) know I've been guilty of that before. I remember being at a worship gathering with a group of Christian friends that I would consider much more "feelings oriented" than I am. About twenty-five minutes into the worship service, I began to wonder when the singing was going to wrap up and move into the teaching. Little did I know, we were just getting started. The singing portion of the service went for nearly an hour before we were seated. When the pastor got up to teach, I was expecting a robust biblical teaching (a minimum of thirty minutes but probably forty to fifty). Instead, the pastor spent ten to fifteen minutes explaining the Holy Spirit had prompted him to spend their time that morning praying for one another. So instead of teaching, we were to gather in groups and pray for one another for the next twenty to thirty minutes. After the service was over, I remember walking away with a sense of superiority, an air of ego that "my church" would never operate like that. We were *much* more rooted in our faith than these people. Instead of giving the benefit of the doubt or learning from these people who earnestly prayed to God (for longer than I had in *weeks,* mind you), I put my defenses up. I could have looked for commonalities. I could have taken the time seriously and invited prayer from these brothers and sisters over the parts of my life that needed God's mighty hand to work. I could have assumed something to the tune of, "I bet they *do* spend time teaching in this church, but maybe, just maybe, today God wanted His people to pray." Instead, I assumed the worst.

Eventually, I repented of my arrogance.

arms crossed

I find I'm not alone in that experience of rolling my eyes and assuming the worst. An "arms crossed" divide can result in the church between the "head" and "heart" people. This divide can be seen between the Reformed and charismatics, the discipleship people and the worship people, and more. We become an army divided instead of an army on mission together.

You may or may not know how far out of control this has gotten in the age of the Internet. People have made entire careers out of ruthlessly rifling through the work and words of Christian leaders, all with one aim in mind: to find any error and publicly call them out. With social media giving everyone a microphone, we have seen every Christian leader and speaker labeled, criticized, and warned against.

While Scripture clearly tells us to discern the truth and to protect the flock, and while it is good for grotesque sin that has hidden in the dark to come to light, it seems that the church in America is facing its own terrible version of a witch hunt. And the most heartbreaking part is that we have many times created unnecessary divisions with our allies.

enemy thrills

The divide of head and heart, and along other divides we will discuss in future chapters, can cause us to put stakes in the ground, refusing various types of growth God might want for us, all so that we might prove our own leaning is the best leaning. As we do this, we naturally harbor suspicion toward anyone who doesn't lean like we do. We recoil from our brothers and sisters instead of coming under the banner of what makes us family to begin with: the blood of Christ. Can you imagine how thrilled the enemy is when that happens? What an effective way to distract us from the cause of Christ! I can hear the words of the enemy now:

> I will make brothers and sisters call one another unbelievers over secondary doctrinal differences.

> I will make small issues big ones for these Christians.

> I will make them blind to the goodness of people on their team.

> I will distract them from their purpose and make them spend their lives pointing out wrongs.

> I will rejoice at the hurt the Christians feel from one another.

> They will miss the real fight against the authorities of darkness because they are too busy fighting one another.

> They will perceive themselves as better than their brothers in their own eyes.

None of us want to be on enemy soil. If we remember whom we are fighting against, we can remember the main things that unite us as brothers and sisters. Perhaps we can help one another see more and more about the One for whose cause we are actually fighting. After all, one of the primary purposes of the church, according to

Paul in Ephesians 3:10, is that "through the church, the manifold wisdom of God should be made known to the rulers and authorities in the heavenly realms" (NIV). This "manifold wisdom of God" is seen when we, in our various facets, all reflect the same multifaceted God who unites us!

Did you catch what happens when do we do this? When we reach arms across and together display our multifaceted God, it's not just the world that looks in wonder; it's all the heavenly rulers and authorities. The church of God, together reflecting the diverse glory of God, is something both angels and demons can't look away from. It makes a statement to both heaven and earth about who God is. All because we chose to be unified as a whole, our multifaceted God is made known.

We have to remain humble and have curiosity for how God is using us all to shape our view of Him. Maybe the ways the other streams are approaching Him aren't always leading to a dead end. It could even be that they are seeing parts of the same beautiful whole.

look at the moon

Think about the way we see the moon. Each day the moon is the same. But each day you might personally get a glimpse of a different part of the moon in your view. Your exact view might vary according to your location, the weather, and whatever instrument you are using.

Similarly, we are all viewing new facets of the same big God every day. There are legitimate areas of caution here because you will hear some say things about the moon, but you realize they are actually looking at Venus. When some people talking about Jesus are contradicting what He says in Scripture, you know they can't be talking about the same God you are. It's only loving to say, "Gaze over here with me. . . . That's Venus, but here is the moon."

Many times, though, we are just experiencing different facets of God in different moments. There is always more to see. There is a way to be both inquisitive and humble as we learn more about the amazing expanse of His kingdom from people who might have had a different vantage point. And if by chance they *are* getting it wrong, we can relax when we come from the posture of knowing we are *all* on a journey toward loving God with all of ourselves. After all, at one time in our life we got some things wrong, too. And on some points we will probably get it wrong yet again. This does not mean we never correct someone, but rather we do the good work of correction gently, just as we would want someone to handle us (Gal. 6:1).

Every day we are given this amazing opportunity to worship the same God in increasingly whole ways.

integration—to love Him wholly

At this point you may agree in theory—*sure, I should love God with both my head and my heart. But how?* How do we *actually* integrate the head and heart? If we want to live less segmented and more whole lives, we must know the answer to this question.

One of the most insightful and helpful answers came from our study of the original words of the great commandment, *that we are to love the Lord our God with all our heart, with all our soul, and with all our mind.*

We talk in this chapter about "mind" and "heart" based on our common modern understanding of those words. We have spoken about them based on our preconceived definitions with the mind associated with *thinking* and the heart with *feeling*. The study of the Hebrew words, however, reveals something interesting, a major overlap in the biblical definitions of the two words.

Let's begin by looking at the great commandment where it first appears, in Deuteronomy 6. In the commandment, we are called to love God with all of our heart, all of our soul, and all of our might. Interestingly enough, you'll see that the word *mind* isn't included in the commandment as originally written in Deuteronomy (the word *mind* doesn't appear until the New Testament).

If you're like me, you're troubled, thinking, *Wait! Why isn't the mind included in the passage? Was it left out by accident? What's going on?*

The Old Testament writers, writing from an ancient Israelite mind-set, actually viewed the mind and the heart as one. They innately believed that our thinking, our emotion, and our desire were interconnected and integrated parts of our humanity. As it turns out, what we constantly try to divorce has been married together from the beginning.

This becomes clearer when we look at the Hebrew word *lev*, which is translated as "heart." The word *lev* has a wide range of meaning, and although translated "heart," it includes many of the functions we associate with our mind. For example, human imagination and intellect are a part of the heart. Also, human understanding, decision making, and wisdom are a part of the heart. So, from the ancient Hebrew mindset, when the command is given to love God with all of our heart, it actually includes functions of the mind such as intellect, decision making, and logic, in addition to our emotions, feelings, and desires.[5]

This messes with us, doesn't it? It challenges the reasons we define the words *mind* and *heart* the way we do in our modern language. But it actually proves the point that these core parts of ourselves are so intertwined that you can't parse them out.

While we, in our modern Western mindset, tend to separate mind and heart into two different parts of who we are as humans, the biblical writers had a much more holistic view of what it means to be human. The reason this is so helpful to us is because it allows us to see that God's command for us to love Him with all of our heart is an invitation to learn to love Him in ways that don't always come most naturally to us. It's an invitation for "thinkers" to learn to love Him with their emotions, feelings, and desires. It's an invitation for "feelers" to learn to love Him with their thinking, processing, and decision making. It's an invitation to love God as wholly, integrated human beings. To study Him and to experience Him. To know Him and to love Him. All at the same time.

In essence, God is saying: *"Just take everything about you, all of who you are, and love Me with that."*

He made us in our entirety, He knows us in our entirety, and He wants us in our entirety.

Perhaps the greatest way we can practice loving God in an integrated way is by NOT trying so hard. It takes too much energy to parse ourselves out, untangle all that we are into subcategories, or give God only the segments of ourselves we are most confident about. In fact, as we are learning, we can't actually segment ourselves as we wish we could. We may have assumed the mind and the heart could be divorced, but as it turns out, they are forever married. They aren't the problem. They've been trying to work together. We're the ones that have tried to separate them, and so we must cease pulling them apart, take a breath, and just come to God as we are—a mess that cannot be untangled or rightly examined, layer by layer, by anyone but Him. That's the answer for how to combine the head and heart: just come with all that you are. If your thoughts are out of control, just bring them to God. If your feelings are bouncing around, don't shove them down; just bring them to God too.

In our journey of doing this, we will naturally look for an example. Who can show us how to worship the Father in a way that is whole? His Son Jesus, of course. Christ showed us how He loved His Father with all of His mind and all of His heart.

Jesus was a mind person

Have you ever thought about the fact that Jesus was a learner?

Yes, He was God. But He was also human, and He willingly chose to live His life in a man's body and grow in wisdom alongside His fellow humans.

Consider this passage, describing a moment in Jesus's childhood:

> **The boy [Jesus] grew up and became strong, filled with wisdom, and God's grace was on him.**
> Every year his parents traveled to Jerusalem for the Passover Festival. When he was twelve years old, they went up according to the custom of the festival. After those days were over, as they were returning, the boy Jesus stayed behind in Jerusalem, but his parents did not know it. Assuming he was in the traveling party, they went a day's journey. Then they began looking for him among their relatives and friends. When they did not find him, they returned to Jerusalem to search for him. After three days, **they found him in the temple sitting among the teachers, listening to them and asking them questions**. And all those who heard him were astounded at his understanding and his answers. When his parents saw him, they were astonished, and his mother said to him, "Son, why have you treated us like this? Your father and I have been anxiously searching for you."

> "Why were you searching for me?" he asked them.
> "Didn't you know that it was necessary for me to be in
> my Father's house?" But they did not understand what
> he said to them.
> Then he went down with them and came to Nazareth
> and **was obedient to them**. His mother kept all these
> things in her heart. **And Jesus increased in wisdom
> and stature, and in favor with God and with people.**
> (Luke 2:40–52, emphasis added)

This passage shows us clearly that Jesus actually *grew in wisdom*.
He was committed and He *learned* like any human. As He was physically growing, He also had to grow in His knowledge of God. He had
to learn to love God with His mind. Do you see how it happens? Do
you see how He went to the temple—how He *listened* to what was
taught from the Scriptures, and how He *asked* questions? The Son
of God—who made the world, who is called the Wisdom of God
(1 Cor. 1:24), who knows no need of teaching because He knows all
things—chose to come to earth, become a man, and in His humanity *learn*. And Scripture doesn't just say He learned His Hebrew Bible.
No. He learned obedience too: "Although he was the Son, he learned
obedience from what he suffered" (Heb. 5:8). Imagine that: God in
the flesh learning obedience.

Jesus was fully God, but we also have to remember that He was
also fully human—a human who had to learn to understand the
Scriptures and to obey them. Just like you and me. Jesus modeled
for us perfectly what it looks like for a human being to love God
with all of his mind. And if Jesus had to learn to lean toward God in
His mind, shouldn't we?

Jesus was a heart person

We are probably comfortable with the fact that Jesus had knowledge, but we might picture Him being distant or removed from

the *emotions* of humanity. But the affections of Jesus were not disconnected from His thoughts and beliefs.

Not only did Jesus show great concern for the emotions of the people around Him, but He also displayed emotion Himself.

- When faced with the death of His friend Lazarus and the weeping crowd around Him— right before He resurrects Lazarus from the dead—we see that Jesus wept (John 11:30-46).

- A death within an individual, personal friendship was not where Jesus stopped. He cried for His entire people, too. When looking at the unrepentant hearts of His people in Jerusalem, tears fell from His eyes (Luke 19:41-44). His own people were visited by the One who could save them, and they did not know it, and instead of welcoming Him, they put Him to death. The thought of their missed opportunity broke the heart of Christ.

- When attempting to take time for solitude and a crowd interrupts Him, He felt compassion for their sick and healed them (Matt. 14:13-14).

- When wrestling with His own call to die, He offered up tearful, loud cries and petitions to the Father (Heb. 5:7).

Note that in these examples Jesus does not just *act* in compassion or *respond well* to grief. He *experiences feelings* of compassion and grief. Note also that He doesn't keep these feelings to Himself. Jesus's emotional life and His thought life are both engaged *with His Father* and *with people* during His time on earth.

A lot of us have thought that maturity means distance from emotion. But it's important to remember that Jesus, while being fully man and full of God's power, expressed emotion while never being in sin. There isn't a lot of reflection within the church on Jesus's emotional life, but we see it clearly when we search the Scriptures. The heart and emotions of Jesus are not segmented from but are perfectly united to the mind of Jesus. Again, Jesus modeled for us, perfectly, what it looks like for a human being to love God, and come to God, with all of his heart.

learning to love

I (Kathryn) started seeing pictures of a more holistic relationship with Jesus after I headed off to the University of Arkansas as a freshman in college. I already knew how to talk about God, how to read the Bible, and how to pray, but I still kept him at a distance. No one ever seemed to notice.

That was until I met Michelle.

Michelle literally chased me down one day as I was walking into the lobby of the Humphries Dorm. She introduced herself to me and said she was on staff with Campus Crusade for Christ. I wasn't really interested in pursuing a relationship with her because I felt it might affect the cool persona I was trying to build my freshman year. (I didn't make it far with that.) And, if I'm being totally honest, my past was filled with so much Bible study, so much "small group" time, and so much church that I was burned out and currently enjoying a break from it all.

Michelle didn't give up on me though. She continued to reach out, whether that meant inviting me to Sonic or having me over to her house. Our friendship grew. I helped her decorate her nursery, and she helped me cram for exams.

I began to learn about God in a way that didn't feel like class. If it did relate to class, this was definitely less of a lecture and more of a lab. She recognized the one-dimensional nature of my faith in Jesus and wasn't afraid to call me to more. It didn't take her long to see that underneath the surface I was a big mess. It turns out, my head and heart were divided.

My heart was a mess because it was trying to do a few things at once. For one, my heart wanted independence because it was dis-trusting, due to my parents' divorce. Underneath that desire for independence, of course, was just a whole lot of hurt. And on top of all this, I was trying to nurse that wound by putting my heart somewhere I thought it could recover and be loved—unhealthy relationships with guys. My heart was trying to run and trying to recover from a wound and trying to fill a void, all at the same time.

But all the while, my mind knew I needed to be with believers and in the Word. So I did that too. I even served in my campus ministry. Some might say I was living two lives at once, and I guess I was. But at the same time, I think what was really going on is that I had divided my mind and my heart. Or perhaps I should say I was ignoring my heart while tending to what I was "supposed to do" with my head.

Have you ever been there—a season of major disconnect between two parts of yourself?

Michelle helped me bridge the gap between the two. It was time to come to God with not just my mind but also the mess of my feel-ings. He already saw them. He could handle them. After all, He's the one who built them into the human experience.

It was time to pursue God wholly in all of my life. I had to give Him the anger that was about to explode in major ways. I had to take Him up on His promise that my heart could safely open up to Him.

I could no longer segment myself and pretend faith was only for a classroom outside of my actual, real life.

I began to confess sin. And not just sin. The suffering too. I laid out all of my pain and worst feelings, and I began to beg God for new desires. I asked Him to change my heart to line up with my head. I asked Him to heal the parts that were wounded. And over time, thankfully, He did just that.

I began to experience a hunger for extended time with Him. I was devouring Scripture and desired to practice the presence of God in every moment. I was experiencing Him in class, and in nature, and even with my friends at parties. *It was true....* There *was* more than just knowing about God. I didn't know it at the time, but what I was experiencing was this: as I began to relate to God in *all* of life, I was learning to *love* Him. And truly trust Him.

This had to happen outside the church building for me to know it was real. I don't know if many people feel that way, but for me it did. It's not that what happens on Sunday isn't a miracle; it is. But carrying it with you to the rest of the week, to the rest of all your days and moments—that's a miracle too. One I hadn't experienced till that season of my life. Life with God happens in both spaces, not just one. And I just wonder if more of us began to fully show up to God outside the walls of the church, if we would see the power of Christ in greater measure *within* the walls on Sunday mornings. It's something to ponder.

thinking again

Frustratingly, it's easy to slip in and out of settling for experiencing less of God, even after we learn there is more. I found myself there again after college, after I got married and had four babies, one after another.

My husband, BJ, and I joined a small group of married couples in our church. We did Bible studies. I found my spiritual life again being formed mainly by traditional church structures. Though I loved my church and my community, I found myself falling into numbness in my faith again, sleepwalking really, and I missed the days of spiritual vibrancy I had experienced in college.

It was so hard to be backtracking. I told my friend Jennie I thought this stage of life was meant for boredom, that maybe we shouldn't expect to be spiritually alive like we were in college now that we were "real adults."

I reverted back to what I had always known to do, which was to use my mind. I would jump-start my faith by learning as much as I could. I depended on everything offered to me at the church building or whatever was newest on the Christian bookstore shelves to prop me up spiritually in that season. Sunday, for me, was a lecture. Bible studies were full of desks and whiteboards, places I knew I could be competent.

Over time I left the various church programs often wondering what I was missing in the rest of life. . . . I wanted God to be bigger than He was in my mind at the time, and I knew from experience that He was. I knew He could show up in my real life. I needed Him to. And so I prayed for Him to break me out of the small box I had put Him in all over again.

And so it is with us as humans. We slip back. We unlearn. We forget. But God is faithful and continues to present Himself to us over and over again, unwilling to let us settle for less than everything He has for us. He helps us remember.

head spinning

There is a passage I must have skipped over for much of my Christian life. When I read it during this stage of my adult life, it took me about a month to digest it, but it helped me understand how my way of relating to God—even in adulthood, after all I had learned!—was not complete.

It is from John 5, and in it Jesus is speaking truth into the lives of the Pharisees. The Pharisees were careful students of the Jewish law. They wanted to obey the law and were well versed in the Scriptures. Their minds were engaged with the information there, to the point that they were able to correct anyone around them who wasn't as well-versed.

To these students of the Scriptures, Jesus said something that made my head spin.

> You search the Scriptures because you think that in them you have eternal life; and it is they that bear witness about me, yet you refuse to come to me that you may have life. (John 5:39–40 ESV)

This was mind-boggling. For a large part of my Christian journey, I thought the whole point was to search Scripture and eventually reach a pinnacle of biblical understanding. I thought in the Scriptures—and knowing enough of it—I'd find true life. And isn't the Scripture full of life-living help? Isn't it full of principles we should dig into, as if they are hidden treasure? How in the world can Jesus say we can be mistaken about Scripture's ability to impart life? And yet here are His words, plain as day.

This verse, in the moment I needed it most, gave me exactly the epiphany I needed.

I realized I could know the Scriptures but not know Jesus.

Andrew Wilson, in his book *Unbreakable*, says it like this: *"Because the Bible is God's Word to us, and because of its beauty and power and richness and depth, it is possible to think that it is the Bible which gives life, rather than Jesus. It is possible for our hearts, restless idol-factories that they are, to take one of God's greatest gifts and accidentally make a god out of it."* [6]

Was my head knowledge increasing again but my heart's love remaining stagnant? Was it possible I had been learning the Bible but missing Jesus, the man the whole thing pointed to? Could I be merely turning pages and not *walking* with Christ?

an uninformed mind

Maybe you can relate to my previous experience, a growing knowledge of who God is and yet a heart's love for Him that remains dormant.

Or maybe you can't. Maybe your experience has been the exact opposite. Maybe your relationship with God has been kindled through times of passionate worship, long prayer sessions with friends, and slow walks in nature that allow you to soak up His presence.

If that sounds familiar, there's also a chance that there have been seasons of your life where your emotions have gotten the best of you. Perhaps they led you the wrong direction a time or two. Or circled around you in seasons of despair or darkness in ways that felt inescapable—like they were your master instead of the other way around. Emotions can tend to do that sometimes. If we're not careful, those of us who most easily relate to God from our hearts can allow our emotions to take over our lives like waves crashing over a ship without a captain.

The thing about emotions is this: *they don't need to be ignored; they need to be informed.*

Emotions are not bad or wrong in and of themselves; quite the opposite, actually. To be a human being is to have emotions. They are helpful indicators of what's going on inside if we pay attention to them. But unchecked emotions—or better said, *uninformed emotions*—run wild and cause all sorts of problems. From a biblical perspective, the psalmist David offers incredible insight on how to inform our emotions.

David's prayers in Psalms are great examples of what it looks like to relate to God with your whole heart. We see David express all sorts of emotion as he writes. He cries, vents, seethes with anger, grieves, repents, stands in wonder, and rejoices—all in one book of the Bible. Yet, in many of his prayers, he returns to what he *knows* about *who God is* in the midst of all these feelings. He feels all the feels, *and* he reminds himself of the truth about God's character all in one session of prayer.

But how could David have known about who God is? Where did he learn of the Lord's character?

We might say it's because he had experienced the Lord showing up for him in past seasons. That's true! But if you look closely at many of his psalms, David points to God's character as seen in various experiences he himself never went through. He points to the past stories of his people, to the creation narrative at the beginning, and to the Law. All things that came down the pike before he was even born.

So, if David points to these things—things that were not born out of his own experience—as a way to inform his emotions, how did he know about them?

He learned them. With his mind. He had an informed mind through knowledge of the Hebrew Scriptures.

In other words, the reason David can pause in the middle of the flurry of his "feels" and not be completely overcome by emotion is because *he knew his Bible.* If David hadn't known his Bible, he'd have little knowledge of God to cling to in the hard times. He may have had just the small experiences of God in his own lifetime to cling to, but then again, would he have even called out to the God of Israel in the first place if he hadn't known the stories of this God's faithfulness in the generations before him? Probably not. Without knowing what came before him, and the Scripture that chronicled such precious information about his God, he would have no anchor of knowledge to inform all the waves of emotions encircling him. He'd be left reeling with nothing to reorient or ground him. And if he wasn't careful, he would have ended up pouring his heart out to an unknown God. Praise God that David knew what it meant to worship God with both head and heart.

If you're an emotional person, take heart in David's example. Be encouraged that David models what it looks like to go to God with the fullness of his emotions day after day, even writing down his wrestlings. Had David ignored his emotions, he would have missed out on what it means to walk with God through both the valley and the mountain. We would have missed out as well because we wouldn't have any of those psalms! If David didn't relate to God in these "heart" ways, all that knowledge in David's Bible would have stayed on the shelf instead of touching down in David's real life. And don't you want the knowledge of God to touch down in your real life?

David's example shows us how powerful it can be when a heart person wrestles not only with how they feel but also with what they *know.* He shows us that we don't have to choose—an integrated person isn't only able to consider their emotive state but is also able to reason with themselves. There are times they fully feel the waves of their emotions before God, with no other agenda, and other times they stop and inform their emotions with the truth—truth that has the power to tell the heart what to do with itself when it's all over the place (Ps. 43:5)!

a beautiful integration

The God who created our intellect also created our emotions. In fact, while one study shows that we have around six thousand thoughts a day, another shows that we experience about two thousand different emotions during a day.[7]

What would it look like to give them all back to Him as an offering of worship? With nothing withheld? Did you even know God wants you to do this? That He welcomes it? What could that even look like?

Take a look at this picture of this beautiful and mysterious combination of the simultaneous pursuit of knowledge and love expressed in this prayer in Ephesians:

> I pray that you, being rooted and established in love,
> may have power, together with all the Lord's holy
> people, to **grasp** how **wide and long and high and
> deep is the love of Christ**, and to **know this love** that
> surpasses knowledge—that you may be filled to the
> measure of all the fullness of God. (Eph. 3:17–19 NIV,
> emphasis added)

These verses say so much about how God invites us to come with all of ourselves.

1. Not only will we spend a lifetime trying to **help our minds grasp** his infinite love . . .

2. But as we understand the width (it's for so many of us) and depth (it reaches down to the deepest parts of each of us) and length (it lasts for all of time . . . He's not leaving us) of this love, how can it not **captivate our hearts**?

3. When our hearts are sufficiently awakened to that reality, we will again want to **know this love** . . . to literally know more about it. We will want to know more about Him.

4. And still we must know that this knowledge of His love is surpassed by **love itself**.

We could spend the rest of our lives trying to digest and live out just these verses. It's so much to absorb! At the very least, we are left with the reminder that God is inviting us into a beautiful integrated life with Him, a breathing out of all we feel as we inhale every ounce there is to know about our Savior. **He wants no less than for us to be filled to the measure of all the fullness of God.**

a heart awakened

My husband BJ had been a self-proclaimed "mind person" until he decided this year that he was going to start approaching Scripture for more than information. He is a history expert and always approached the Bible with intrigue but digested its information in much the same way he did history books. He decided to ask God not just to help him learn but to *meet with him* through Scripture.

One simple change BJ made (which, by the way, he wouldn't say this is *the* change other people have to make in order to experience God but was simply something that helped him) was to slow down in his Scripture intake. While he still valued the skill of studying the Bible and still tackled huge passages of Scripture in order to understand certain verses in context, he added a skill to his set: meditating on one verse. As he rotated this practice into his Bible intake routine, he began to sit with the Word and journal about what the Lord might be showing him personally. He prayed for an awareness of His presence. He began to sense God was there with him, speaking to him. He articulates all of this with tears in his eyes. And to a mind person, tears are often unusual.

He began to tell the kids the difference he was feeling . . . that instead of only learning about God, he was *relating* to Him as he would a person or a friend. And the most amazing thing of all is that the growth he's having with the Lord is translating to those around him as well. He's learning to love the Lord not only with his mind but also with his heart. His emotions with us, his family, are suddenly more real—or perhaps I should say *fuller*—as well. And I'm sure that's the reason the next verse after loving God in the great commandment is about loving other people. One leads to the other.

All the factors in BJ's life were leading him to being in the box of only worshipping God with his mind for the rest of his life. This is what his denomination would have leaned toward, this is what his personal family life would have steered him toward, and this is where his personal learning style and personality profile would have kept him. But this is the thing about the Lord: He is relentlessly in pursuit of all of us, and He can trump any of these factors, and He will if we let Him. He wants all of us, and He wants us to pursue Him with all of ourselves. As James K. A. Smith says, *"Jesus is a teacher who doesn't just inform our intellect but forms our very loves. He isn't content to simply deposit new ideas into your mind; he is after nothing less than your wants, your loves, your longings."*[8]

BJ has been formed. In fact, he has impacted countless people as of late that relate to his story. His story so vividly demonstrates the fruit of living out the Great Commandment: that we are to love God with the fullness of our beings, our intellect and our emotion, not holding any part of ourselves back from the God who made us. We don't want anything less. And neither does God.

a mind awakened

If you're a heart person and you wonder what leaning toward God more with your head could look like, consider our friend Kathy, who is also naturally a heart person. She had grown up in a church that never really opened the Bible, but she loved prayer and relationship with God from an early age. Like BJ, so many factors in her life could have sealed the deal that she'd remain in the same place for the rest of her life. But God wanted more than just her heart. He worked in her life, and eventually she realized she didn't know much truth about who God actually is. Instead of remaining uncertain about what Scripture had to say about the God she had pursued with her whole heart, Kathy pursued learning her Bible.

It felt like an overwhelming task.

Kathy heard a speaker give an overview of the Bible that gave her the overall narrative of Scripture. God's purposes in the Bible began to make sense in new ways. Kathy continued to study, and she grew in her knowledge of Scripture. Because she is such a people person, she couldn't help but share her enthusiasm for what she was learning. Soon she was gathering groups of friends together to meet and discuss the things she was discovering for the first time. Finally, she set out on a journey to write her own Bible overview to teach women. Over the next three years she created her own tool for just that purpose.

Many people would say their lives are affected, either directly or indirectly, by my friend Kathy. I think it's because she already loved God with all of her heart and soul, but now she is also on the journey to love Him more and more with her mind. She is acquainted with the God of the Bible. She says she now knows who He actually is.

Taken together, Kathy worships God (and ministers to others in His name) with a heart ever stirring and a mind ever growing. If you asked her about life before this phase, she'd tell you—she'd never go back. Because there's nothing like relating to God with every part of who you are.

I don't know if you relate more to Kathy or BJ, but just imagine what the greater church could be like if we followed their lead.

all that we are

As we mentioned, it seems the Lord is telling us through the great commandment: *"Just take everything about you, all of who you are, and love Me with that."*

The end goal of all we are learning about God can't be knowledge itself but must be the love of God. And at the same time, the end goal of all that we feel in a worship experience can't be the roller coaster of emotions themselves (as if spiritual moments are not real unless they are explosive or sensationalized) but rather meeting with the God of the Bible Himself—a God we can actually describe.

> *Our learning must lead to love.*
>
> *On the other hand, our love should lead to learning.*

As we wrap this section up, think about a romantic relationship. When you love someone, you automatically have the insatiable desire to know more about them. You might find yourself looking through all their pictures on Instagram. Your ears perk up if someone is describing a situation when they interacted with them. You ask them questions. . . . You desire to know more and more about who they are because you love them. Your love leads to learning.

In the same way, a real love for Jesus (not a feel-good-quasi-Jesus we make up in our heads) leads to a desire to know even more about Him. And yet one of the clearest ways to know Him is to read His Word, to study it, to memorize it, and to let it transform us. John 14:21 says: "The one who has my commands and keeps them is the one who loves me. And the one who loves me will be loved by my Father. I also will love him and will reveal myself to him."

We keep his commands because we know them in the first place. We know them because we read about them. We read about them because we have made time to put them in our minds.

On the other hand, if we start learning more about Jesus, we should naturally want to do all of life with Him. Our desire for Him will grow, and we'll want to relate to Him with more and more of ourselves. Our learning should lead to loving Him with all of ourselves.

Some would argue that it should all start with love. Some would argue that it starts with learning. I would argue that it doesn't matter where it starts, rather that we lean toward Him with whatever part of us we're holding back. That we grow where we're weak, and we keep going where we're strong. That we don't ever stop growing in fullness of relationship with Him so that we make it over the long haul in our life with Him. After all, a lot is at stake both here and for eternity.

moving forward together

We experience God's delight as He takes the areas we don't feel secure in and helps us grow. We become whole, in both immeasurable knowledge and immeasurable love for Him. Instead of having to choose how we will relate to Him, we can pursue without abandon loving Him with our all. And I meant to say *without abandon*. In many Christian books, you'll hear of pursuing God with abandon, meaning, you leave all else behind for His sake. And there's truth to that, if you think about the ways we're called to leave our idols behind, or our "old self" behind with its worldly ways. But when I say without abandon, I mean you don't have to abandon any category that makes you human when you come to God. We can come, with ALL our hearts, as He says. ALL our minds. If we have a posture of learning and humility both personally and corporately, living out the great commandment is actually possible. *Enjoyably* possible.

So, what can you expect to see if you dare to relate to God with both your head and your heart?

This is where it gets exciting.

first, expect to experience more of the abundant life Jesus promises is possible

As cofounders of our ministry, Dwell, we hear the question often, "Is there more?"

This question bothers some because they think it might be referring to Jesus not being enough. And when it comes to His death and resurrection being enough to save us from our life of sin, He is certainly enough. However, when it comes to the way we relate to Him for the rest of our time on earth, there is *always more.* Jesus "is the same yesterday, today, and forever" (Heb. 13:8). Our love and knowledge of Him, though, is ever expanding by the work of the Spirit. The fact that we change from glory to glory proves there's always more down the road for us to learn, for us to enjoy, for us to repent of, for us to be surprised by.

I've seen this up close over and over again. The other morning I sat with my neighbors, who are in their seventies, on their back porch. In recent years they had been in a dry spot spiritually. And yet suddenly they informed me that they had entered a new season where they were now growing in their love and devotion to Jesus more than they had in decades. You know what they had done? They just started praying for a deeper love for Him. They were in the Word, but instead of just reading to deposit information, they started asking God to meet with them there. He had answered. They were amazed.

You can be too.

Tears were shed in that morning conversation, and I left with the hope that there is always more and more abundance of life with Christ around the bend. We have the opportunity to keep getting more of God.

second, expect to see growth in the lives of those around you

Our son Andrew watched his dad describe the opening of his heart and emotions toward the God of the universe for the first time in his forties. As I watched this interaction, I thought, *This moment could shape our son's life forever.*

Especially in the lives of men, heart integration can be a decades-long journey, and many never get there. If my husband hadn't been open to praying for growth, Andrew would have potentially grown up thinking emotions were bad and not a part of our communication with God. Now he knows God wants his heart and all his days, not just his Bible study time.

I can't imagine the benefit this will be for not only Andrew's own current life but for his future life as well. His future wife, if God wills. His future kids, if God wills. His future ministry and work relationships and neighborhood chats—all this and more will be massively impacted by one person's choice to relate to God with the part he was holding back.

The same is true for you, friend. Just imagine who might be impacted by your one brave choice to offer up to God both your head and your heart.

third, you can expect to better give God the fullness of love He deserves

When God gives us a commandment and says, "This is the most important thing I can tell you to do," it's worthwhile to give that thing some focus, right?

He repeated again and again that the first thing we should do is to love Him with all that we have, every piece of us—with all of our thoughts, all of our emotions, all of ourselves. Does the Maker of our whole being deserve a love that encompasses all of who we are? Absolutely He does, especially when He says it's our highest calling. So let's not withhold an ounce of ourselves from Him.

You can obey the greatest commandment. You can offer Him the love He deserves—the love you've probably been trying to give Him, but partially. You can see your life truly poured out as an offering the way you've always longed to do, alongside David and BJ and Kathy and so many others who are learning to pull certain parts of themselves out of hiding and into the light.

a whole way of loving God

There's open terrain before us—let's grow toward integration of the mind and heart as we identify our own leanings and learn from the leanings of others. Where do you lean?

if you're a heart person . . .

Could one or more of these help expand the way you relate to God?

- Identify some areas of insecurity you might have around your scriptural knowledge and pray over them.

- Consider asking a mentor to meet with you who is clearly a gifted student of the Word.

- Consider finding an overview of the Bible or an in-depth study that challenges you to think more deeply. Consider doing this in a group study, in fact, so you'll have others to help you along in the journey of knowledge.

if you're a head person . . .

Could these ideas expand the way you relate to God?

- Start the practice of describing your actual emotions to the Lord when you come to Him in prayer. Let Him in. Tell Him how you feel and what's going on in your day.

- Instead of conquering big amounts of Scripture when you open it, consider meditating on one verse and asking the Lord to meet with you there. Have a conversation with Him as you would a friend.

- Consider asking to meet with a mentor who is more of a heart person.

a prayer for mind and heart

Here's a prayer that is modeled after an ancient liturgy in the church. It emerged from a desire that we all, together, awake from apathy as we move into loving God with all of ourselves.

O Lord, hear my prayer.

From my apathy about the things of Your kingdom,
Deliver me, Jesus.
From my undisciplined nature,
Deliver me, Jesus.
From my choices to stay guarded,
Deliver me, Jesus.
From my blindness to your plan,
Deliver me, Jesus.
From ears deaf to Your voice,
Deliver me, Jesus.
From a will that wanders from Yours,
Deliver me, Jesus.
From my heart that settles for less of You,
Deliver me, Jesus.

For an awakening from my sleepy state,
Give me the grace to desire it.
For a hunger for Your Word,
Give me the grace to desire it.
For a thirst to know who You are,
Give me the grace to desire it.
For sight to see beyond the temporal,
Give me the grace to desire it.
For a readiness to hear Your whispering voice,
Give me the grace to desire it.
For the conviction to pursue You with my mind,
Give me the grace to desire it.
For a longing heart that desires you above all,
Give me the grace to desire it.

Amen.

section 2 :// spirit + truth

It was a normal Tuesday afternoon, and I [Aaron] was sitting in my usual spot in one of the old, yet nicely kept, Ouachita Baptist University classrooms. I always sat on the far left side of the room, second row back, next to one of the old windows that overlooked the campus plaza. I was ten weeks into my senior-level Christian theology class. I remember being uncertain about that particular class going into the semester. My uncertainty was partly due to intimidation, another part a strong case of senioritis, all mixed with a strong hatred toward a few particular guys in the class who seemed to find extreme enjoyment in picking theological fights with anyone and everyone willing to tolerate them. Yet, much to my surprise, in just the first few class sessions, I almost immediately fell in love with studying theology.

As the weeks passed by, portions of the reading and teaching affirmed and deepened some of my previously held theological convictions. I remember feeling confident studying certain topics like the doctrine of justification, the inspiration of the Scriptures, and the resurrection of Jesus.

And then, again to my surprise, other portions of the class really challenged me, revealing how shallow and even unbiblical my thinking was in some areas. I can recall with vivid accuracy a moment when we began looking at ecclesiology, a theological term that means "the study of the church." For the first time I realized that almost all of my *strong* opinions were nothing more than overly confident, college-kid personal preferences. I was greatly challenged to rethink my views about what the church is and what the church could look like.

But as I think back on that semester, I can say without a doubt, the most surprising moment for me was not the affirmation of already held beliefs or the exposure of my weaker areas of theology.

The most surprising moment for me was when I realized there was an entire category that I knew *nothing* about . . . the Holy Spirit.

I grew up in a wonderful church. It was a small Missionary Baptist church in an equally small town in southern Arkansas. In my early years my parents took me to church regularly. Our family was engaged in the life of our church. I was, at best, disinterested yet compliant with "all things church." I was running after all of the wrong things at that point in my life. I found girls, sports, and nearly everything else more interesting than Jesus.

That was until I started to get a good taste of the bitterness of the fruit of rebellion.

Caught in lies. Burned by unhealthy relationships. One Sunday evening I found myself exhausted, heartbroken, and quite frankly, completely done with it all. The weight of guilt lay heavy on my shoulders. Shame felt as tangible as the old church pew I was sitting on. There, in the back of that church sanctuary, I met Jesus. It's probably more accurate to say that Jesus met me there that evening. I did little other than come to the end of myself and, in complete desperation, call out to Him to help me, to save me. Although my encounter with Jesus that evening wasn't as dramatic as the apostle Paul's blinding experience, for me it was just as life altering.

Almost immediately I noticed a change in my desires. It wasn't that my old desires completely went away; it was just that I had new desires that were equally strong. Suddenly I wanted to please God with my life. I asked my mom to buy me a Bible. I still remember her taking me to Mardel Christian Bookstore and letting me pick out a large leather-bound NIV Study Bible. She even bought me one of those old-school Bible cases that held a couple of pens, had room for a journal, and zipped closed. I'm laughing about how ridiculous I looked lugging that big thing everywhere I went, even now as I type this. But the silver lining was that it made me feel serious about my faith in Christ, and that was important.

In my youth group I began to lead worship and write songs. Within a matter of months some friends and I had formed a band, written some of our own worship songs, and begun to travel to lead worship at various small-town church events. Eventually, by the time we were in college, that band grew, and we found ourselves leading conferences, large student gatherings, and weekly college worship nights on our campus.

Over those years leading worship, I began to grow in my understanding of what it means to worship God, to serve Him and His people, and to use the gifts He has given me.

As we traveled from event to event leading worship and ministering in different contexts, I consistently found that when my life was surrendered to God and His purposes, He was always faithful to use what seemed to me to be a feeble offering, to accomplish purposes that far exceeded my gifting.

During those early years of following Jesus, I remember a number of moments where God seemed to work supernaturally in my life. For example, there were many moments where I was on stage and had a deep sense that I needed to say something, yet I didn't know exactly what to say. In those moments as I stepped out into the unknown, oftentimes scared to death, and spoke to the people, suddenly, almost out of nowhere, words would come to me almost as if God Himself was supplying them.

In other instances, I remember praying prior to worship gatherings and deeply sensing that God wanted to work in a particular or special way that evening. In several of those moments, I would somehow visualize in my mind's eye particular events happening. And then, nearly without fail, I would step out and lead, and the exact scenario I previously visualized in prayer would happen as I had seen it.

The only way I knew how to summarize this was to say that Jesus seemed to provide opportunity after opportunity for me to advance His kingdom in ways that corresponded directly to how He has uniquely gifted me to serve. He then not only provided the opportunity, but He also empowered me and gifted me, at times supernaturally, to accomplish the task. And in those certain moments, it seemed that He wanted to give me advance notice so that I was ready and didn't miss what He was doing.

This brings me back to that Tuesday afternoon in my Christian theology class.

I sat, jaw dropped, as I listened to my theology professor explain who the Holy Spirit is and how the Spirit works within God's people to bring about God's purposes. To say this was a time-stands-still moment for me would be an understatement. It was as if my professor was giving me vocabulary to explain so much of what I had experienced in my life as a Christian up to that point. I began to understand that the Spirit empowers and gifts God's people for ministry, which is exactly what I had been experiencing.

In an almost eerie, yet wonderfully remarkable way, my professor was introducing me to Someone I already knew well. It was as if I had been close friends with someone to the point that I had come to trust them deeply, yet I had never met them face-to-face.

In those moments, I realized the incredible accuracy of the Scriptures regarding the Holy Spirit. What I had been personally experiencing through the Holy Spirit was exactly what the Bible teaches to be true of the Spirit.

In the days and weeks following this newfound understanding of the Holy Spirit, one question kept surfacing in my mind over and over: "How could I have completely missed something, Someone, so central to the Christian faith?"

spirit or truth

Over the next few years, following my personal awakening to who the Holy Spirit is, I also began to learn that everyone did not look so fondly toward the Spirit and the "things of the Spirit." Possibly even more surprising to me, I sensed an extreme emphasis on the importance of the Bible in some camps to the point that they almost never talked about the importance of the Spirit, while other camps did the opposite—putting the Holy Spirit in the highest place of prominence while almost never pointing to the importance of the Bible. As if there was a good reason to choose or decide which one must be valued most. That seemed strange to me.

I then learned, as we discovered in the last section of this book, that depending on which church someone grew up in largely deter-mined which side of that debate they typically fell on. Again, it was odd to me that many Christians either preferred to trust the Bible or the Holy Spirit to guide them, but few, at least in my circles, trusted both as equally important to the work of God in their lives.

As I looked around, I could find solid Bible-teaching churches who knew the Scriptures well and submitted themselves to the authority of God's Word, yet many of those churches seemed to lack spiritual fervor and often fell into religious legalism. On the other hand, I could find churches that emphasized being Spirit led and empowered that felt alive and vibrant in spiritual life yet often seemed to lack a high value for the written Word.

Few seemed to reflect what Jesus was calling us to in John 4:24:

> "God is Spirit, and those who worship him must worship in Spirit *and* in truth." (emphasis added)

This Scripture gives us a clear call to worship God in both Spirit and in truth.

So, why is this yet another area we often separate?

realizing our gaps

When we talk about separating the Spirit of God and the Word of God, we must stop and admit the obvious: they can't actually be separated. It is impossible for us be filled with the truth and not filled with the Spirit. Nor can a person be filled with the Spirit but not the truth. Yet in our worship practices, we can act as if the two are separated. We can act as if we are only filled with one. We can neglect one or the other. And where separations happen, gaps emerge.

Some of you have a *truth gap*. For those of you who have been in church for some time, this can be a shameful secret.

You still don't know the Bible.

Sure, you know stories and you know verses, but you get nervous if asked too many questions. You are afraid you will be exposed at some point, and your deficiencies will leave you vulnerable. So you fake it in Bible conversations instead of asking questions. You subconsciously decide you are not smart enough to learn it, and you stop trying. You live with the shameful secret that you don't know the Bible, and you lean on others to be the "Bible people."

Or you might come from a community that has emphasized prophecy and fresh messages from the Lord, but you've never stopped to think about the value of learning the *already* revealed Word of God in the Scriptures that has been written not just for the "Bible types" out there but for *you*. You've missed out on the riches and the grounding the Scriptures provide you. This truth gap limits you because it keeps you from growing in understanding of, as we mentioned in the last section, who the Lord actually *is*.

Or maybe you're in another stream, one that flows with great Bible-teaching churches. You can recite Scripture, maybe even teach it. You have a well-rounded theology, maybe even a strong theology of the Spirit, but in reality you still have a *Spirit gap*. You might relate to Wilson's words: *"Some of us, as a result of our personalities and backgrounds, can find the Scriptures easier to manage than the Holy Spirit."*[9] For reasons we will explore more in this section, you might even be facing the fact that:

- You have quenched the Spirit (1 Thess. 5:19 NIV).
- You've resisted Him (Acts 7:51).
- You've neglected Him (1 Cor. 2:14).
- You've grieved Him (Eph. 4:30).
- Or you may have even despised Him (Luke 12:10).

There are so many reasons we become comfortable with our gaps and shy away from growing in either Spirit or truth. Often, at the bottom of it all, significant fears underlie our lack of integration.

fear of extremes

Let's take a closer look at why you and I may be approaching "the other side" with fear and suspicion.

Many in the charismatic stream seem to be at home worshipping God in Spirit, looking at the people in the "truth camp" with bewilderment. If you are there, you might feel like the "truth people" are neglecting their relationship with God by intellectualizing the faith. Sam Storms articulates this well in his book, *Practicing the Power*. He says, *"Charismatics tend to fear relational distance. They want nothing to do with impersonal religion that relegates God to a remote and deistic heaven."*[10] If you're a Spirit person, you wonder if people in the other camp have a relationship with God at all. You wonder if there is actual faith, actual dynamic relationship, actual growth.

However, for people coming from the truth stream, Storms articulates that there can be a *"fear of excessive familiarity with God . . . and a concern that we will get too chummy with God."*[11] If you're in the truth stream, you might wonder if the Spirit people have any deep reverence for God at all or respect for His written Word. You might also wonder if your brothers and sisters have a relationship with the actual Jesus, or if they are, at times, making up a version of Him that's not true to the Scriptures. They might seem weird and flighty. You wonder if they are just following whims and emotions.

Deep down, most of us have some legitimate fears about the "other side." We've all heard stories of things going awry. Many times we have suspicion about those in other camps because we have seen legitimate abuses of the things they say they hold most dear.

We have seen abuses of the Spirit. We have also seen abuses of the Word.

We've seen spiritual gifts manipulated and flaunted. We've seen people who pull the God card and put a "thus saith the Lord" in their mouth when, really, they simply want permission to pursue their fleshly desires, all under the guise of "the Spirit told me this or that."

We've also seen the Word taught incorrectly and carelessly. We've seen the Bible used just as manipulatively by shepherds to strong-arm their sheep into their fleshly plans or even to cover up evil all in the name of "the Bible says."

We've seen both the Spirit *and* the Word used for personal gain rather than the edification of the church. But this is an interesting thought: although we can all admit we've seen **both** Spirit and truth mishandled, we often will choose to draw close to one and distance ourselves from the other. According to our camp of choice and also our bent, sometimes we pick the camp where we aren't going to allow people to make mistakes.

From the Spirit camp:

> Oh, I've seen people teach through the Word verse
> by verse, but so often they have misinterpreted and
> misguided people as they taught. And that's not to
> mention there's no power in so much of their teaching.
> And wasn't that true of the Pharisees? All that Scripture
> coming out of their mouths, and yet no real faith or
> power or life change. I'm going to stick to being more
> of a Spirit person. The Spirit will lead us into truth. The
> Spirit will awaken us to life and change us!

If this same person saw the spiritual gifts "going wrong" in the life of one of their friends within their tribe, they would have much more patience for that. They would extend a generous spirit and the benefit of the doubt to help the friend grow. But subpar, or seemingly lifeless Bible teaching? That's easy to throw out. And there is little tolerance for making mistakes.

From the truth camp:

> I've heard people prophesy and hear from God, and I feel like it was totally made up. I've seen weird things on TV and heard stories about people "hearing from God," and these are things He would never say! I'm sticking with TRUTH!

If it involved missteps in teaching the Scripture, that person might be willing to come alongside a fellow teacher and say, "Hey, way to step into your gifting and give it a go. We can learn together as you grow . . . even when you make mistakes!" He would have patience with others in the learning process as they explore how to rightly handle God's Word. But in exploring the guidance or gifts of the Spirit? This person would likely show little tolerance for mistakes, no room for imperfections as we learn.

Storms has a term for this whole experience. He calls it the "Eleventh Commandment of Bible-Believing Evangelicalism," which basically goes like this: *"Thou shalt not do at all what others do badly."*[12] And he's right. Fear of extremes and worst-case scenarios can keep us not only far apart from one another in the body of Christ; it can also keep us from personally growing in both Spirit and truth.

Have you approached things this way? Do you refuse to grow where you aren't comfortable or where you've seen other people make mistakes? Do you fail to offer the same generosity of spirit, or benefit of the doubt, to "their" side as you do your own? Are you tempted to completely reject something when you see someone else doing it wrongly, or even just immaturely? Do the mistakes of others, seen from afar, make you think your only option is to dismiss "that" particular stream of Christians altogether? Have you thrown the baby out with the bathwater?

learning from one another

Sure, growth might feel vulnerable or unsafe for us if our entire spiritual identity is built on the Christian stream we find ourselves in, and especially if all our relationships tend to fall within our "camp." However, listening to one another across streams might be one of the most helpful exercises in spiritual growth we could practice, and it has the potential to bring about unity in the church at large, which is desperately needed.

We need a new wave of humility in this era of the church. How much different would we be if we realized how small we are in the grand scheme of things and how large the family of God is, globally speaking—a grand body made up of many, many streams? How much different would the church at large be if each of us committed to give grace to people who get things wrong sometimes, knowing we are probably getting that much or more wrong ourselves? What might change in our churches and in our country if we remembered that our theological insights, habits of worship, and ways of doing things are part of the whole, but they are not the only way? To become more spiritually mature in these ways, we might need, for a moment, to quiet our fears and suspicions and ask God to help us see people outside our stream of the church with His eyes.

One way you might grow to better integrate "Spirit and truth" in your life is to start making friends outside your smaller circles. Read their books. Listen to their podcasts. Maybe you don't agree with every word, but what if you didn't cut them off immediately? What if you didn't reflexively assume the worst but, instead, chose to assume you need them and they need you, like wood needs a flame to make a fire?

embodied beliefs

Before we continue, we want to pause and reflect on where we are as it relates to worshipping God in Spirit and truth. We need to be clear: we aren't talking about where we wish we were. We aren't talking about where we are on paper. We are talking about what our lives actually reveal about our beliefs.

For instance, plenty of people say they believe in the importance of the Word, but they spend no time in it. Confessionally, they believe in it and might even say they love it; functionally they do not. Their time tells on them—it exposes the true beliefs that lie underneath their professed beliefs. As for the existence, presence, and power of the Spirit, plenty of people say they believe in this too. But if they do not act as if He truly exists or invite His power into their actual life (and the life of their church), whether that means asking Him to empower their ministry or help them fight sin regularly or open their minds to the meaning of Scripture or guide them in their deci- sions, do they *really* believe in His power?

First Corinthians 4:20 says, "For the kingdom of God does not con- sist in talk but in power" (ESV).

God doesn't want us only to sit around and speculate about the importance of His Word but never immerse ourselves in its pages. He also wants us to do more than simply assent to, or speculate about, the Spirit's presence and power in our lives.

Where are you satisfied with simply *agreeing* to a certain set of Christian doctrines but not *embodying* them? Are you satisfied with claiming the Book but not living by it? Or even knowing it? Are you content with having lots of discourse about a theology of the Spirit but not *walking* by His power or actually *experiencing* His help? No matter which way you land, we are all great at believing things on paper that we don't live in practice.

The temptation is always to give yourself credit in both categories. I don't meet many Bible people who would say they don't believe in the Spirit. And I don't meet many Spirit people who would say the Bible isn't important. But the truth is, *functionally*, we all do a way better job *actually practicing* one or the other.

And so I'd encourage you (and myself!) to get honest about that. Where do you give preference when it comes to your time and attention? Simply put, are you more of a Spirit person or a truth person?

Here are some general questions that might help you discover how you lean:

Are you more of a "truth person"?	*Or a "Spirit person"?*
You love to read and study Scripture.	You love to sit and listen in prayer.
It's important to you to understand who God is.	It's important to you to know God intimately.
You love talking about theology.	You love talking about spirituality.
You prefer accuracy.	You enjoy mystery.

You emphasize God's Word when making decisions. You desire to see God's power poured out in our generation, and you emphasize hearing from God in a felt way when making decisions.

bonfires

While we have many reasons to stay disintegrated, potential growth awaits us. If we are willing to integrate Spirit and truth, we'll find it is life changing. We cannot let our present culture of polarization, the divided streams of church history, or our personal leanings keep us from the fullness of what is offered to us in Christ.

Here is a helpful word picture, revealing the importance of both Spirit and truth in the lives of Jesus's followers.

Imagine in your mind, a large **bonfire**.

The truth is the wood: strong, stable, foundational. One hundred percent necessary for the effectiveness of the fire.

The Spirit is the flame: the ignition, constantly moving, full of power. One hundred percent necessary for the effectiveness of the fire.

We could easily and proudly stand beside our stack of dry logs and say, "Well, that's it! I did a great job building this!" We could talk about how the logs are stronger and more stable than the flame all day long. After a while, though, we would look down and realize the logs have grown moldy. They are still stable, and they definitely don't put anyone at risk. Anyone would look at them, however, and say that they were built for more.

We could also stand proudly beside the power of the flame. I am picturing just holding the button down on one of those BIC lighters. We could say, "*This* is what the bonfire is about! The FIRE! We don't need anything else! This is where the power is!" But after a while, in reality, the flame will die because there is no stability underneath it.

Any of us can see how the bonfire is incomplete without the foundation of the wood or the power of the flame. But we struggle to realize that it is the same within our own spiritual lives. If you're hungry for growth, if you want to see more people know and love Jesus, then you need to hear this:

You need the power found when God's **Spirit** not only illuminates His **truth** in your mind but also empowers you to live it out in your life.

Remember, much of the growth in our spiritual lives is based on integration. Jesus said that true worshippers worship Him in truth **and** in Spirit. We need to be Bible people—people who increasingly value, know, and live out God's Word all the days of our lives. And we also need to be Spirit people—people who are empowered, gifted, and sent out by God to display His love and reveal His kingdom on the earth.

We need the wood. We need the flame.

filled with the spirit + grounded in truth

We are taught in multiple places throughout the Scriptures about the importance of the Spirit and truth.

In a beautiful passage in the book of Ephesians, Paul is instructing the believers in Ephesus on how to follow Christ's example, walking in the way of love and living with wisdom. He writes, "Do not get drunk on wine, which leads to debauchery. Instead, be filled with the Spirit" (Eph. 5:18 NIV).

I find Paul's logic here fascinating. According to his understanding, for the Ephesian believers to walk in love and live with wisdom, they need to learn what it means to be "filled with the Spirit." One might naturally assume that Paul would have suggested they read some helpful books or take notes from wise teachers from the past in order to learn this way of living. Instead, Paul ties the believers ability to follow Christ's example directly to being filled with the Spirit.

Paul knows that human effort alone is futile and lacking, but when God's people are filled with His Spirit, they are empowered to walk in His ways and live in a way that glorifies the Father.

The command Paul gives to "be filled" is both a present and an ongoing command. Paul is teaching the believers that much like a lake is continually refilled by the streams that empty into it, so we can be ongoingly refilled by the Spirit. This does not mean the Spirit is only partially deposited at our conversion, nor does it mean that being regularly filled with the Spirit makes us more and more saved. We receive the Holy Spirit in our conversion; every believer has the Spirit indwelling inside. Receiving Him happens at the moment we are saved, but He still desires to continually fill us and empower us for communion with God, righteous living, and more effective ministry. We have Him already, *and* we can be ongoingly filled with Him. Or, as J. D. Greear puts it, *"One baptism, at salvation. But many fillings."*[13] For you and me to begin to live a more integrated life, we too must listen to Paul's teaching and learn what it means to be filled with the Spirit. Let's together ask the Father to fill us to overflow.

The Spirit, however, is not all that we desire to be filled with, for we also ought to long for the Word of God to fill us. In fact, one of the ways the Spirit fills us is through our reading of the Scriptures. In another of Paul's New Testament letters, as he is writing to young Timothy, he says this,

> From childhood you have been acquainted with the sacred writings, which are able to make you wise for salvation through faith in Christ Jesus. All Scripture is breathed out by God and profitable for teaching, for reproof, for correction, and for training in righteousness, that the man of God may be complete, equipped for every good work. (2 Tim. 3:15–17 ESV)

In context, Paul is instructing Timothy on what it looks like to live amid godlessness. Paul stresses the necessity and sufficiency of the Scriptures in Timothy's life. According to his understanding, the Scriptures are necessary for every aspect of a believer's life, beginning with the initial wisdom required for salvation, until he or she is completely mature and equipped for every good work. In other words, unless we have a love and devotion to God as displayed through our commitment to consuming the Scriptures, we are destined to remain spiritually immature. For you and me to live a more integrated life, we must press into the gift that is ours in the Bible.

Jesus was a Bible person

When it comes to what it looks like to live a life in Spirit and truth, Jesus Himself is our north star: the clearest example of what it looks like to glorify God. So let's see how Jesus beautifully exhibits what it looks like to worship His Father in truth. As we look at this aspect of His life, note that Jesus is unique in this regard because He both *knows* God's Word and also *is* God's Word. John said it this way in the opening of his Gospel:

> In the beginning was the Word, and the Word was with God, and the Word was God. He was with God in the beginning. (John 1:1–2)

When John refers to the "Word" in this passage, he is not referring to the written Word of God in the Scriptures; he is referring to Jesus Himself. This is important for us to recognize for a couple of reasons: (1) Because it is incredibly powerful for us to realize that the living Word of God Himself held high the written Word of God in His own earthly life. (2) And to note that in this chapter when we refer to the "Word of God," we are referencing the written Word of God, the Holy Scriptures. We do this not to minimize the fact that Jesus *is* the Word but to spotlight Jesus's deep devotion to the Scriptures.

As previously mentioned in the last section of this book, the Gospel writers paint a picture of young Jesus as a grower in His knowledge of and teaching of the Torah.

Once He began teaching, Jesus repeatedly demonstrated His love for the Scriptures and the divine authority He believed them to hold. He quoted or referenced different passages in the Old Testament forty-nine times, and several of these He repeated often. He quoted from Genesis, Exodus, Leviticus, Deuteronomy, Psalms, Proverbs, Isaiah, Jeremiah, Ezekiel, Daniel, Hosea, Amos, Jonah, Micah, and Malachi.[14]

But Jesus didn't just *know* the Scriptures. We see Him draw from the power of the Scriptures again and again in difficult situations. In Matthew 4, we see Jesus led by the Spirit into the wilderness to be tempted by the devil. He had been fasting forty days and nights when the devil asked Him to turn stones into bread. Jesus's method of spiritual warfare in this moment was to recall the Scriptures and rebuke His enemy with the truth of God. He responds, "It is written: 'Man shall not live on bread alone, but on every word that comes from the mouth of God'" (v. 4 NIV).

Another example of Jesus's personal love and devotion to the Scripture is when He was on the cross, just moments before His death. In that dire moment, Jesus's choice of words came from Psalm 22, an Old Testament passage that specifically prophesied His death and the moments He was living. "My God, my God, why have you forsaken me?" (v. 1 NIV).

As we take a close look at Jesus's life, we see that He knows, loves, teaches, and prays the Bible. And in some of the most trying times of His life, when He could have done absolutely anything, He draws upon the words of the Scriptures as His power and strength. All this because He dedicated *years* to opening it up and taking it in.

For all of His life—from the start of His life to the years of His adult public ministry to His dying breath—Jesus was the purest depiction of a Bible person.

Jesus was a Spirit person

Now that we've seen clear examples of Jesus modeling what it looks like to value the authority and truth of the Scriptures, let's also look at how He modeled being a Spirit-led human being. And, similar to the caveats we offered above regarding Jesus being the incarnate Word, we must give a quick caveat here as well when it comes to the Spirit. The Son of God and the Spirit of God's relationship finds itself within the Trinity. As we know, the Son of God is the second person of the Trinity, and the Spirit is the third, both fully and equally divine. So in a sense we are mingling with mystery when we talk about their inner relations, which have existed from eternity past, before the Son of God ever took on human flesh in the person of Jesus. But for the purposes of this section, we are specifically exploring Jesus's relational interactions, *in His humanity*, with the Holy Spirit. While Jesus is much more than merely our example in this life, He is not less than that, and we can learn much from the way He, in His human nature, followed the leading of the Holy Spirit.

Wildly enough, we can actually observe the connection between the Holy Spirit and the person of Jesus before Christ was even born. **Prior to His birth, the biblical authors foretold that Jesus would be recognized as the One upon whom the Spirit rests.**

Read the prophet Isaiah's words about Jesus's coming, written approximately seven hundred years before his birth.

> A shoot will come up from the stump of Jesse;
> from his roots a Branch will bear fruit.
> The Spirit of the LORD will rest on him—
> the Spirit of wisdom and of understanding,

the Spirit of counsel and of might,
the Spirit of the knowledge and fear of the LORD.
(Isa. 11:1–2 NIV)

In essence, as Isaiah is delivering the good news that a Messiah is coming to bring salvation to the world, he is saying that one of the ways the Messiah will be recognized is by the Spirit of the Lord *resting* on Him. The Spirit did not come and go throughout Jesus's life and ministry, as we see with various people throughout the Old Testament. Rather, Jesus was the One who modeled what it looks like to listen to, receive guidance from, and obey the Holy Spirit. Jesus was the perfect resting place for the Spirit of God.

Once Jesus was born, which was a miracle of the Spirit's power in and of itself, His life and ministry continually revealed what it looks like to live a life glorifying to the Father by the power of the Holy Spirit. At Jesus's baptism we get a glimpse into the Father, Son, and Holy Spirit working as one. When John baptized Him, the Spirit descended physically, identifying Jesus as the Messiah. Luke records what took place as follows: "The Holy Spirit descended on him in a physical appearance like a dove. And a voice came from heaven: 'You are my beloved Son; with you I am well-pleased'" (Luke 3:22).

Shortly after this moment we get a glimpse into Jesus's human nature as He makes His way forward as a Spirit-filled and reliant man. Luke says, "Jesus, full of the Holy Spirit, left the Jordan and was led by the Spirit into the wilderness" (Luke 4:1 NIV).

For the Gospel writer Luke, it isn't happenstance that he is recording these details about Jesus's life. Rather, it's important for Luke to let his readers know that Jesus is the promised Messiah, the one who is fulfilling the Old Testament prophecies, the one on whom the Spirit rests. Luke, guided by the Spirit as he wrote, intentionally makes known that Jesus Himself was *full of the Holy Spirit*. This phrase, "full of the Holy Spirit," refers to an ongoing process of being filled and empowered by the Holy Spirit.

Luke goes on to say in the same verse that the Spirit led Jesus into the wilderness.

I grew up thinking that Jesus lived a perfect life, performed miracles, and never sinned just because He was God. And while that is true—He was and is God—Luke is also showing us here that walking in the power of the Spirit, being continually filled by Him, and submitting to His leadership at every turn is the *only* way to walk in righteousness or do the Christian life. Isn't it wonderful to see that Jesus—yes, even Jesus—in His human nature, willingly submits to the leading of the Holy Spirit in His life? In doing so, He reveals something profound: *that we can entrust our entire lives to the Father through the power of the Holy Spirit.* Jesus did that. Here in this passage He follows the Spirit into the wilderness where He would soon be tested by Satan. Ultimately, the Spirit would lead and empower Jesus to willingly give His life for us on the cross. And then, three days later, Jesus would rise from the dead by the power of the same Spirit (Rom. 8:11).

From Jesus's birth to His death, the Scriptures record many of the instances where Jesus was tempted, entered into ministry, rejoiced in the Father's will, cast out evil, instructed others, healed ailments, and performed good works. And in so many of these cases, the Gospel writers point out that Jesus was doing these things in the power of the Holy Spirit (Luke 4:1, 14; 10:21; Matt. 12:28; Acts 1:2; 10:38). Yes, as we watch His earthly ministry in the Gospels, we know He had a divine nature as God, which we do not have, but He also had a human nature as a man modeling what it looks like to walk by the Spirit of God. He said in Luke 4:18, "The Spirit of the Lord is on me, because he has anointed me to preach good news to the poor."

Yes, it takes time and care to parse out exactly what we can expect to do in the power of the Spirit compared to what only the Son of God can do, but the obvious point is this: Jesus lived the perfect

Spirit-filled life as a human being. He was the purist depiction of what it means to be a Spirit-led man.

missing the mark

Hopefully by now we are beginning to see the potential for life-changing growth that could be ahead for us. Hopefully you are catching a vision for the Spirit-led and truth-filled life that God invites us into and that Jesus modeled perfectly for us. If you are, you might also be wondering, *What are my next steps as I grow? Where do I start, and what are some common mistakes I need to avoid?* We will offer a few words of wisdom that might help as you journey ahead.

First, here's a story to share as we are growing alongside you in our own spiritual integration.

learning to listen

A few months ago I (Kathryn) wanted to continue growing in being led by the Spirit, so I prayed that I would learn to hear the Spirit's voice in greater measure. Life after that intentional prayer has been more interesting for sure. God has spoken in some simple and humble ways—through others, through His Word, and through His still small voice. However, one day was particularly special—a day I sensed the Spirit guide me in a more dramatic way. This marks the day I met Marcus.

The prayers I prayed for the Spirit to clearly lead me weren't on my mind at all when I left lunch with a friend in one of the nicest areas of Little Rock. As I got in my car, about ten feet away from me stood a guy—a tall guy but still with youthful features, just standing there and shivering a bit. I couldn't tell how old he was. I felt the Spirit lead me as I looked at him. "Put him in your car." Let me be clear:

this wasn't an audible voice but simply a nudge I felt that I didn't initiate on my own, and it had a weight to it.

Lord? Is that you?

Peace beyond my own understanding flooded my soul, so I rolled down my window.

"Hi, um, what are you doing out there?" I said.

"Not really anything."

"This is a weird thing to ask, but are you a safe person?"

"Yes ma'am, I am."

"Do you want to get in my car? I can take you where you need to go."

"Yes," he said.

WHAT AM I DOING? Lord?

It was slightly awkward at first, but he responded that he would like some lunch and we pulled through Chick-fil-A. That began a couple hours of conversation with this guy, who turned out to be fifteen years old. Strangely, I didn't have anything planned for that time, and I believe that is because God knew where I needed to be.

I asked Marcus where he was living, and he explained that six weeks earlier he had been thrown out of his house. His mom's boyfriend heard him break a plate, got angry, and his mom couldn't take it. She told him he had to leave and couldn't come back. He had walked twelve miles to the nicest part of town, and he had spent six weeks making a way for himself. I couldn't believe my ears as he explained how he was doing just that.

"Where have you been sleeping?" I asked.

"Under the bridge over there. No other homeless people sleep there. And oh! I used to be a Boy Scout, so you won't believe what I did! I found a trash compactor full of shirts, and since I know how to tie great knots I knotted them all together for a sleeping bag, and it kept me warm."

"Wait, were you out there in the ice storm?"

"Yes ma'am."

Holding back tears ... and anger. "What do you do all day?"

"Well, I realized after a few days that no one was coming to look for me when I got no calls. And then my phone went dead. So I started making a routine for myself. In the mornings I walked to the library ... I knew I should keep my brain sharp. In the afternoons, I walked a mile down the road to a basketball court and found some friends to play ball with. Then before it got dark each day, I would walk back to the bridge. Oh, and I stopped at McDonalds each way, and someone always would buy me meals if I was standing there."

What? How incredible. How brave. Lord, what do you want me to do?

"Do you have any other family?"

"I do have my uncle that lives thirty minutes away, but his number is in my phone, and my phone went dead six weeks ago."

He was so alone.

I can't explain the feeling I had that day with Marcus in my car. I felt such supernatural motherly love for this boy I had never met. But I felt even more than that. I felt like God was with us in the car that day. There was not one other thing on my mind other than continuing to follow the Spirit's guidance that started this whole thing and obeying it at every turn.

We bought clothes, snacks, and a portable charger. Marcus wanted to meet up with his basketball friends. His phone would charge while he was playing. He promised to call his uncle once he was finished playing and let me know his status. After these hours with him, I knew I couldn't move on. Especially because God nudged me again and strongly impressed upon me, again in no certain words, that I wasn't going to move on from him.

Marcus is now part of my family's life, and I can't even begin to tell you just how incredible this kid is. He wants to go to the military. He knows all about computers. He wants to build drones. He wants to build things that go into space. We get to talk about all his dreams when I drive him around, and they are big. I think he will accomplish them.

We are learning from Marcus, and he is learning from us. But when I look at him, I just think, *None of this is work. It doesn't feel like service. It's just following the Spirit's lead.* When Marcus is in our house, I remember that the Spirit's guidance touches down into our "right now," and that whatever He leads us to do, He also *empowers* us to do.

God didn't move to bring the universe into existence, move to beckon His people to return to Him through the mouths of the prophets and apostles, move to send His Son so we might be forever reconciled to Him, and then decide He was going to suddenly stop moving. The Spirit is moving us in the now, for the sake of His kingdom. For the sake of people like Marcus. For the sake of people like you and me, for His purposes that are greater than we can imagine. When was the last time you sensed Him moving *you*?

functional denial

Many of us in the truth camp are in danger of missing these moments of following the Holy Spirit's real-time guidance in our lifetime. It's easy, again, to say we believe the Spirit is still active among those in the world and the church today, while somehow forgetting that *we* are "those in the world" and *we* are "those in the church." It's easy to dismiss His promptings, to quench His work in our hearts and our ministries, to believe the Spirit exists and yet still not be led by Him.

Just as we realized in the "head and heart" chapter, there is a *confessional* aspect to what we say we believe about the Spirit, but we must remember there is also a *functional* aspect to what we say we believe about Him, too. On paper we'll say we believe in God the Holy Spirit as much as we say we believe in God the Father and God the Son. But what do our *real lives* say about our view of God the Spirit? Do we live as if He's not really there? As if He's not really God? As if He doesn't still move in this world? As if the Trinity should really just be . . . binary? As if the things He has done amid His people throughout the Bible—and throughout Christian history—are just made-up stories, having no bearing on our real lives?

If we're honest, the answer might well be yes. When it comes to us and the Spirit, we might need to admit that we're much like Peter was with Christ on the night of his arrest: we'll claim Him in our bold moments, but when the test of real life and real onlookers comes around, we deny Him.

Unfortunately, it's easy to do this. We're comfortable talking about all the miraculous ways the Spirit worked throughout the Bible. We love to rehearse revival stories of the past, where the Spirit fell fresh on generations before us and brought fire back into the hearts of God's people. We celebrate missionary stories where He emboldened His ambassadors to speak His gospel no matter the cost or led them to do things that didn't make sense in the moment but ended up furthering the church in unreached places. We even appreciate the stories of how He works in foreign countries today.

But when we talk about something that is actually proximate, some outworking of the Spirit among us *right here* in our real lives that we didn't plan, we often just *don't know what to do with that.*

We believe in the Spirit in lip service, but in real life we would often rather follow the plan we crafted than invite His power to disrupt it in any way. We've got things working, and we don't need Him to interfere. We don't live with the power of God because we have created tidy lives and we are content to operate without it.

don't scare the guests

We (Aaron and Kathryn) held an event in our large suburban church one weekend that drew people who weren't a part of our usual Sunday services. Our normal Sunday services were orderly and predictable. We didn't have many people who came from outside the neighborhood. But at this event we were praying that the Spirit would wreck our routines and control issues and bring new people and reveal Himself to all of us as God. He did in many ways. Many of them happened behind the scenes and were tame, but one incident was out there for everyone to see.

One of the speakers was leading us in a prayer. Many in the room felt a strong, tangible sense of the Holy Spirit in that moment, but one woman at the back of the room started loudly crying out in a voice that was shrill and concerning. A couple of us ran back to her area of the room, wondering if she was inhabited by a demon, or on drugs, or who knows what else. But when we approached her, we just felt led to pray for her, and she became quiet again.

After the service we heard her story. She had been caring for her husband for two years after he had emerged from a life-altering coma. She had a boy with Down syndrome and was homeschooling him. She, consequently, hadn't been to church in two years. She had been struggling with depression and doubt. Her friends found helpers for her family this particular weekend, and they snuck her off, praying fervently for her healing and for spiritual growth. Her own prayer became that the Lord would show Himself to her again. In that moment of prayer, that's exactly what He did.

She was moved, and her wild-sounding screams were actually worshipful cries saying, "Jesus, thank You! Jesus, help me!"

It was beautiful. It was weird. It was scary. It was definitely outside our norm.

It's easier to be open to how the Spirit might move when it's just theoretical. And we like Him to stay theoretical, don't we? Because we're afraid weird things like this might happen if we open our control-clutching, tightfisted hand that is quenching Him in the moment. After all, we don't want to scare the guests!

It helps to ask ourselves this question: Is there a chasm between the way the Bible describes the ministry of the Spirit and the way we allow Him to minister in my domain?

Should we just leave our beliefs on paper?

I guess it depends on what I am more afraid of: quenching the Spirit or losing my carefully crafted illusion that I'm in control.

chasing fresh wind

At this point, if you're a Spirit person, you might be thinking, *Yeah, those tightfisted Bible people need to let the Spirit in so He can do His thing! Let it rain with His power—in Jesus's name!* But have you ever considered that you, too, might be neglecting much of the Holy Spirit's work? Is it possible that you're not as much of a Spirit person as you thought you were? Could there also be more for you?

Let me explain.

For many reasons, a lot of people who'd classify themselves as Spirit people tend to prefer the fresh wind and the exciting power of the Holy Spirit over other normative and seemingly less exciting ways that He works. We can get so focused on pursuing the miraculous that we neglect the quiet or the ordinary. These quiet works of the Spirit are still miraculous, but because they aren't given as much press time in certain Christian environments, we consider them "less than." Not as important. Boring. Or perhaps totally unknown to some of us.

We tend to care about the gifts of the Spirit—specifically the sensationalized ways the Spirit moves in mass settings, perhaps—but we've put no thought toward the *tons* of other ways He ministers to us in the day-to-day.

What are these "less flashy" ministries of the Spirit to us? It is the Holy Spirit who:

- Regenerates the old, dead heart into a new heart that loves God (Ezek. 36:26-17; Titus 3:5-6; John 3:5-8).
- Convicts us of sin (John 16:8).

- Empowers us to resist temptation, fight the sin, and give no ground to the flesh (Gal. 5:16).

- Illuminates God's Word so that we can understand it (John 14:26; 16:13; 1 Cor. 2:12-14; 1 John 2:27).

- Intercedes on our behalf (Rom. 8:26).

- Comforts, counsels, helps, and advocates for us (John 14:26, see various translations).

- Imparts hope to us on days we might otherwise despair (Rom. 15:13).

- Conforms us into the image of Christ slowly over time (2 Cor. 3:18).

- Helps us remember we are God's children when we forget our identity (Rom. 8:16).

- Sheds the Father's love into our hearts (Rom. 5:5).

- Bears the fruit of good character in us over time (Gal. 5:22-23).

The same Holy Spirit who emboldens God's people to step out courageously also helps us walk in meekness. The same Spirit who moves with striking power also moves in quiet humility, bearing the fruit of solid character in our lives over the long haul and tending to all sorts of our needs.

The wild thing is that these ministries of the Spirit aren't any less miraculous than the more dramatic works of the Spirit. *They are all miracles!* Friend, *it's a miracle* that you're different now from the way you were five years ago—the old self has no power to change in this way. *It's a miracle* that you feel a piercing in your heart when your love gets disordered and misdirected toward something or someone other than God; the fallen human heart, apart from God's Spirit, does not feel such a thing. *It's a miracle* that you understand a little more of the Bible than you did in seasons past; a darkened mind is blind to this kind of understanding without the light of the Spirit. Has it ever hit you that if someone were to ask you if the "Spirit has been moving" in your life, you could point to *any* of this as miraculous evidence that He, indeed, *has* been?

Let's look at this from another angle, through a series of questions, just for good measure, because I want to make sure we recognize with greater understanding the *various* ways the Spirit is active in the lives of believers, apart from some of the typical works we would attribute to Him.

Would you think the Spirit healing someone from some sort of physical sickness is a big deal—that such a work points to His kingdom, one that is full of shalom and wholeness?

I imagine the answer is yes. Okay, but do you also see the Spirit at work when:

- He heals someone from anger or jealousy or gossip?

- He gives someone wisdom to know how to handle themselves in a difficult situation?

- He gives a person the power to hold their tongue in a moment their flesh would typically be sarcastic, rude, or combative against their spouse, friends, or kids?

- He leads people not into seasons of wellness and prosperity but into storms or wilderness seasons, like He did with Christ at the start of His ministry?

- The Bible starts making sense to someone for the first time and they are eager to study it with fresh excitement and spiritual fervor?

If we're not careful, you and I will think these examples of the Spirit's work aren't as big a deal as the more flashy ways He moves, and because of that, we will fail to celebrate them in our faith communities. When we fail to celebrate the more "hidden" ways the Spirit works, we end up over-elevating certain displays of His power, and we ultimately forget that He is *always* working in and among us.

Although you are open to and hungry for the work of the Spirit in your life, you too, may be settling for less and missing out on the fullness of the Holy Spirit—on *all* the Scriptures says about His work. It's possible that you might be falling into your own sort of functional denial, believing on paper that the Spirit ministers in these "less flashy" ways yet neglecting those works in your actual life. It's possible that you deny these other works that He does because all you want from Him is what the culture around you considers His "varsity level stuff."

If you think this might be you, ask yourself, "When was the last time I looked for the seemingly smaller and quieter works of the Spirit in my life?" You might benefit from a deeper Bible study on the fullness of the Holy Spirit's work in the life of the believer so that you can begin to value the full picture of the Spirit's good work in your own life.

And do you see the connection here between the truth and the Spirit? Do you see how much better they work when they go together? As it turns out, *growing as a truth person* helps you be *more* of a Spirit person, not less! As you learn about all the Spirit is in the Scriptures, the fuller your experience will be with Him and the better you'll be at spotting his real-time work in your life so you can give Him glory!

I never knew you

If you're a Spirit person and you need more rationale for why you should lean *more* into truth than you have been, these words from Jesus in Matthew 7:21–27 confront us dead in our tracks:

> Not everyone who says to me, "Lord, Lord," will enter the kingdom of heaven, but only the one who does the will of my Father in heaven. On that day many will say to me, **"Lord, Lord, didn't we prophesy in your name, drive out demons in your name, and do many miracles in your name?"** Then I will announce to them, **"I never knew you.** Depart from me, you lawbreakers!"
> Therefore, everyone who hears these words of mine and acts on them will be like a wise man who built his house on the rock. The rain fell, the rivers rose, and the winds blew and pounded that house. Yet it didn't collapse, because its foundation was on the rock. But everyone who hears these words of mine and doesn't act on them will be like a foolish man who built his house on the sand. The rain fell, the rivers rose, the winds blew and pounded that house, and it collapsed. It collapsed with a great crash. (emphasis added)

These words from Jesus are sobering and should cause us to evaluate our lives. For those of us who identify in the Spirit camp, listen to Jesus's warning here. According to Him, it's entirely possible to prophesy, drive out evil, and perform many miracles in Jesus's name, all while not truly knowing Him!

Remember in the last section of this book, when John 5:39 opened our eyes to the fact that a Scripture-oriented person can know a lot of Bible *but still not know Jesus* (p. 37)? This passage here in Matthew 7 makes a similar point to Spirit-oriented people.

Jesus is trying to show us that it's entirely possible to witness, or even be directly involved in, great supernatural power and *still not know Jesus!* If we make the "works of the Spirit" more important than a relationship to Jesus Himself, we have completely missed the point.

In both of these passages Jesus is showing us the bull's-eye of the Christian faith: *actually knowing, following, and loving Him with all of who we are.* Those of us in the Spirit camp need to ask ourselves these sobering questions, "Do we love the supernatural works of God more than God Himself? Do we seek His power but not His face? Do we always demand His action but rarely sit quietly in His presence?

All in all, you can *appear* as if you belong to Jesus because of your association with things of the Spirit and still not actually belong to Him, just as someone who *appears* as if they belong to God simply because of their knowledge of His Word.

As it turns out, Jesus's words to both truth people and Spirit people cut both ways! We ought to see Jesus's stark words in both of these passages as His loving yet truthful invitation to truly *know* Him.

So, what's the answer? Integrating the two.

Think about it. Truth people, Jesus says, won't come to Him for life because they think they've already found eternal life in their knowledge of the Scriptures. So, who grants life in Christ to the believer? It's the Spirit! The Spirit is the one who regenerates a dead heart! The Spirit is the one who illuminates the Scriptures so it's not just head knowledge but *transformational* in the life and heart of the Christian. **What a truth person needs is the Spirit!**

And as for Spirit people, what does Jesus say in the second section above? What is their hope if they've been trusting in miraculous displays? How can they know they really know Jesus and that He won't cast them out? *Right after* He warns them of the danger, He finishes with this (in essence): *"Therefore,* **hear these words of mine** and *do* them—then you'll be a person with a strong foundation, and when others aren't left standing, *you'll stand* in the end when it's time for Me to claim you."

What are "these words of mine"? They are Jesus's teachings from the Sermon on the Mount (Matt. 5–7).

The Spirit people who are in danger of not truly knowing Christ are given hope; they are given an answer for their predicament: *don't get so transfixed on spectacular displays that you break the law of Christ in other ways. Walk according to all that Jesus teaches us in His Word— those who truly love Him know His commands and obey them. Those who truly love Him cherish His Word and live by it.* Do you see it? Just as the answer for the truth people is the Spirit, the answer for the Spirit people is the truth!

This should leave us fully convinced—the Spirit and the truth must go together. We cannot make it in the Christian life, or to eternal life on the other side, without abiding in *both.*

don't neglect

This passage in Matthew is not the only time you've seen the Bible insisting on both Spirit and truth, is it?

Think about it.

On one hand, if you recall one of the most famous chapters in the Psalms, you'll remember that the Bible rebukes those who feel like Scripture isn't their thing. For those who wander from Scripture, God doesn't mince words:

> You rebuke the insolent, accursed ones, who wander
> from your commandments. (Ps. 119:21 ESV)

This is a wholehearted reprimand to those who find themselves straying from truth. Why is this? Why is the psalmist so passionate about God's people valuing God's truth? It is because the psalmist knows how valuable God's words are. Just three verses prior he prays, "Open my eyes, that I may behold wondrous things out of your law" (v. 18 ESV). And just a few verses after that he prays, "Turn my eyes from looking at worthless things; and give me life in your ways" (v. 37 ESV).

The psalmist has tasted the sweetness of the Lord's commands and knows that life and death hang in the balance. He knows that truth revealed in the Scriptures leads away from "worthless things" and to life.

If you're a Spirit person, I bet you've cried out to God to show you the way, or make a way, at some point—perhaps in your family or your church or your personal struggles. I bet you've begged Him for clarity—to lead you away from what He doesn't want for you and *toward* what He has set you apart for.

The beautiful and refreshing reminder for you is that *His Word* does this for you, through the Spirit's illumination! So many times we are looking for wisdom, searching for the good life, or seeking practical guidance for our daily lives, yet we are unwilling to search the Scriptures for divine revelation.

The question is: *Are you willing to dive in? Are you willing to take the time it requires to hear from God in His Word—a way that might feel slower but is always sure and substantial?*

Many would rather have a shortcut. We'd rather hear a fast or fresh word when we are uncertain about something, cutting through the time it takes to hear what Scripture has already said—and has been saying for thousands of years—on the matter. Here's the great news, friend: God's written revelation has guided every generation of Jesus's followers for thousands of years. *And that doesn't mean the Spirit isn't involved.* The Holy Spirit is the One who carried along the writers of the Bible, preserved the Bible through the centuries, and illuminates it to you, helping you hear it and apply it to your life in fresh ways today. So often we want to bypass God's written revelation to us. Don't. If you want revelation, seek the Lord through the Scriptures. It is right there, waiting for you.

While the Scriptures are sacred, sometimes complex, they are always life giving. May we learn to say alongside the psalmist that God's Word is "sweeter than honey" (Ps. 119:103) to our lips, so much so that we find ourselves thinking about it when we rise in the morning and even in the watches of the night.

a powerful integration

I'm convinced the most difficult part of relating to God in the Spirit and truth is the *and.* We've seen the Scriptures call us to both, we've seen Jesus model both, and we've taken a close look at why we tend to choose one over the other instead of *and.* The reality for us is this: the only way to move toward greater integration is to embrace the *and.* Embracing *and* will almost certainly be uncomfortable. Growth always is. Embracing *and* will most likely lead us to face some of our fears (or critics!). It almost always does. But embracing *and* will inevitably lead us toward the life-changing power of God that we are so hungry for.

So, what could it look like to undergird the power of the Spirit with the inspired truth of God's Word? What could it look like for us to also fan into flame the Spirit of God who, if we are His followers, already resides in us? What does it look like to live lives that are like a roaring bonfire, enflamed by the Spirit and built on truth?

It looks like real transformation.

You might say, "I just want balance in my life."

But Jesus is not asking for balance. He is not asking us to know 50 percent of the truth and walk in 50 percent of the Spirit. If we're not careful, in an effort to live a balanced life, we will settle for deficient lives. He's not asking for this sort of bland, predictable, vanilla Christianity in our lives or in our churches. The world won't be compelled by that kind of segmented and impoverished faith. Jesus doesn't want balance for you. He wants transformation.

If you're ready to delve into a life filled with 100 percent truth and 100 percent Spirit, fasten your seat belts. It won't go unnoticed. It likely won't be boring. You can't map out a successful ten-year plan for it. It will affect your life, and it will affect the lives around you.

God has expressly given us some ability to either restrict or release what the Spirit does in our own lives and even in the lives of our communities. Meaning, we can either quench Him with a tight fist, or we can loosen our grip and cooperate with what He's trying to do. God has also given us the choice to either receive with joy or neglect in laziness the power of His written Word in our lives and communities. We can either learn it and come under it, exploring and receiving its riches, or we can act like it's not the treasure trove God says it is—which leaves us not only missing out but also calling God a liar. But if we commit to *both*? If we get on board with *and*? Man. We will be transformed by the living Word and living Spirit in ways that might just wake things to life in the sleepy hallways of the nominal church.

Can you imagine? Spirit people will start worshipping Him in truth. Truth people will start worshipping Him in Spirit. The people of God informed, indwelt, inflamed?

That's a church I want to be a part of. And it's a church the world needs.

moving forward together

As we move forward together, we are praying for Spirit-led and truth-filled believers to rise up and live with both humility and power, meekness and boldness, sacrifice and strength. The only way we can do that is by living in Spirit and truth.

what can you expect as you move forward, together with others, in Spirit and truth

First, you can expect to grow in greater intimacy with Jesus. Relating to God in Spirit and truth will bring new life and vitality to our faith. We will realize once again, or maybe for the first time, that Jesus Himself is the prize.

Second, you can expect to feel "out of the box" within our stream of Christianity. There's a strong chance we will stick out in our circles as we grow in the areas that haven't felt normative to our churches and communities. That's okay and it is a good thing.

Third, expect other spiritually hungry people to find you. Many people are restless and desiring more in their lives with God. It might not happen overnight, but all of our communities have pockets of spiritually hungry people, and over time you will find each other. They will realize there's this *wholeness* to you, and they will want it for themselves. Sometimes they will come in the form of other Christians who are still living in one side to the exclusion of the other. Other times they will be spiritually interested unbelievers. Either way, expect others to be curious and to draw near!

a whole way to worship God

Lastly, what might it look like, specifically, for you to grow toward integration of Spirit and truth? Here are some practical considerations:

if you're a truth person, consider this:

Could one or more of these help expand the way you relate to God?

- Spend some time studying what the Word says about life in the Spirit.

- If you are trapped in fear and confusion, pray for a softening and loosening of a pharisaical spirit, and ask God to help you see what He wants you to see in His Word.

- Pray bigger prayers, or maybe even just more *specific* prayers, believing in His power, and see how He responds.

- Ask God to move you from extreme fear to earnest desire.

- Get to know someone who is more comfortable with things of the Spirit than you are.

- Ask God to make you more sensitive to the Spirit's promptings in your everyday life. Ask Him to help you not just *believe* He is the guide and helper of God's people but *experience* this guidance and help in ordinary moments.

- Square anything you experience, or anything you learn from others, against Scripture. Remember that you're not *giving up* Scripture to learn more about the Spirit. They work together. The Spirit of God will never be at odds with the Word of God.

if you're a Spirit person, consider this:

Could these expand the way you relate to God?

- Read the Bible daily and spend a season memorizing passages of Scripture, or join a Bible study with a group that values theology or doctrine.

- Always test the spirits, as Hebrews says. Don't just trust your intuition or a new fad that certain circles are embracing without inspection or careful thought.

- Take time to pray and discern God's voice more clearly, measuring it against Scripture.

- Get to know someone who knows the Bible better than you do.

- Pray for a desire to grow in ways that might be outside of your traditions.

- Ask God for perseverance as you try to learn the Bible. There will be days when you feel like you are facing a lot of reading, or you may encounter confusing parts. That's okay. There will be days when studying requires flipping around between various resources. That's okay too. It's all part of the process, and the Spirit's ability to provide you with endurance will get you through.

- Remember the Bible is one big story about God and what He's done for His people. Yes, there are many parts, but when you dive into one section, it's a section that belongs in the greater whole.

a breath prayer for wholeness

[breathe in]

> *We are filled with thanks, Father,*
> *that You made every part of us for Your purposes.*

[breathe out]

> *We bring our physical bodies—our hands, our feet,*
> *our whole selves, to You. You created us and*
> *we will follow you, Jesus, with our whole lives.*

[breathe in]

> *We are grateful to You, Spirit, that You see*
> *to the depths of our being.*

[breathe out]

> *We bring our souls and every secret part*
> *of us to You, oh God. You see us, we are known, and we*
> *are safe in You. Open our eyes to all of who You are, Lord.*

section 3 : // being + doing

George Müller wasn't your average spiritual leader. In the mid 1800s in England, he became broadly known as a man of constant and effective prayer, as well as a man on an active and inspiring mission.

After a childhood marked by rebellion, Müller was invited to a Bible study and was surprised he had the desire to go. "It was to me as if I had found something after which I had been seeking all my life long," he said. The group read the Bible, sang, prayed, and read a printed sermon. To his amazement, Müller said, "This made a deep impression on me. I was happy; though if I had been asked why I was happy, I could not have clearly explained it. I have not the least doubt that on that evening God began a work of grace in me, . . . and that evening was the turning point in my life."[15]

For the next four years Müller grew in what he would have described as a deep communion with God. His time spent *being with* God would inform the rest of his life and ministry. Müller soon had the deep desire to share this deep inner work with the people around him, so he became a pastor.

Not long after he became a pastor, God began drawing Müller into a specific mission for the kingdom. God began drawing his heart to the orphan. He was heartbroken after learning there were accommodations for only thirty-six hundred orphans in all of England, with many more orphans needing homes.

At this point in Müller's story, he was faced with a unique choice: Should he pursue sharing the deep inner work God was doing in him, or should he actively pursue the mission to the orphans God was putting on his heart? Which was more important, inner spiritual development or outward obedience in the world?

Simply put, should he live a life of *being* or *doing*?

being or doing

The question Müller faced at that moment in his life is familiar to many followers of Jesus. The Scriptures teach the importance and necessity of both abiding with Christ and living out His mission to the world. Yet, for some reason, the church has often struggled with the tension between our *inner* formation and our *outward* mission. Which is more important—to intentionally withdraw to secret places in order to be with God or to passionately go into the darkest places of our world carrying the good news of Jesus to the lost? Is one of these *more* important?

We believe our answer to this question is critically important, so important, it could possibly determine the long-term health and effective witness of any follower of Jesus or a local church. As we begin to unpack this more, let's start by gaining a better understanding of some of the reasons we tend to have a difficult time integrating *being and doing.*

we all lean

Our tendency to lean, seen in our previous chapters, continues to be a factor when it comes to *being and doing.* We all naturally lean toward lifestyles that are more or less active, more or less social, and more or less cause driven. As we've stated previously, our natural leanings aren't good or bad, right or wrong . . . they're just *how we are.*

Odds are, if you are the type of person who is naturally wired to be more introverted—a deep thinker and someone who loves large amounts of time by yourself—then you might also gravitate toward the *being* side of the spiritual life. Spiritual practices such as silence and solitude, Scripture meditation, and prayer walks will have a more natural appeal to you. Many of our friends who lean this way reveal what's most important to them in conversation as they talk about what it means to learn to rest in the abiding love of God. They are often quick to bring up how great the need is for each of us to learn to *be with God* without an agenda or a checklist, valuing Him for who He is as much as what He can do for us. Those who lean toward *being* know that the inner formation of the Christ follower is absolutely central to what it means to follow Jesus. After all, how can we be changed by Him if we spend no time in His presence?

In contrast, those who are naturally wired to be helpful when others are in need might gravitate toward the *doing* side of the spiritual life. Spiritual practices such as serving others' physical needs, rallying others toward missional projects, community service endeavors, heading up ministries in the church, and sharing the gospel in unreached places fires them up! If you ask about how God is at work in this person's life, they are quick to talk not about their time in the prayer closet but about the tangible ways they see God at work through the projects and initiatives they are involved in. Their eyes are more fine-tuned to see God moving in the outward ways. The ministry is growing. The neighbor became a Christian. The pot-luck or soup kitchen was a success. If you hang around this sort of person long enough, you'll hear them passionately share about the needs they see in the world and the importance of sharing the gospel so that the world might come to know Christ. This sort of personality often shakes others out of their complacency, toward the mission God has invited us into. For many who lean toward *doing*, the outward mission is most central to what it means to follow Jesus. After all, if we are God's people and we believe God is up to redemptive things in the world, how can we not be a part of it?

So, what about you? What do you think about the way your personality leans? Do you focus more on inner and personal spiritual growth, or are you more motivated by carrying your kingdom mission to the world? Are you more of a be-er or a doer?

Are you more of a doer?	Or a be-er?
You love moving fast.	You prefer a slow pace.
You love action.	You love rest.
You value efficiency.	You value quality time.
You love missional endeavors.	You value solitude.
You fear wasting time.	You fear getting overwhelmed.
You have a hard time saying no to invitations.	You have a hard time saying yes.
You hurry a lot.	You embrace quiet.
Your task list distracts you during your time with God.	In your daily quiet time with God, you linger.

We have to look at ourselves objectively again: Are our personality leanings shaping the ways we relate to God? Of course they are.

And they don't just shape us. They shape things bigger than us, too.

churches lean

As has been the case, if we step back and take a look, our churches and denominations often have a leaning toward being or doing as well.

There's no way for me to know what kind of church you grew up in (or attend now), but I bet it either focused most of its messaging and energy catering to your personal, individual, internal growth journey with Jesus, to help you better sit in God's presence on a daily basis and become the best possible version of yourself, *or it spent most of its effort funneling you into its many outward-facing initiatives of good works in the community, to share the love of Christ with a lost and broken world.*

If the former, my guess is that you heard a lot of sermons about getting alone with God, becoming a prayer warrior, listening to God in the quiet place, or taking the time to pull away and receive the promises of God that are rightly yours to claim in His Word. In short, it's all about *me and Jesus.*

While a lot of that is well and good, the hidden danger for these types of churches is that they become so focused on developing ways to grow with Jesus on the internal, individual level that they forget not only the corporate dynamics of being a Christian but the external mission of God that also comes with being a faithful disciple of Jesus.

On the other hand, if you had the latter experience, you probably heard a *lot* about the needs of other people. Sermons were probably about being Jesus's hands and feet to a desperate world, getting unsaved people saved, enlisting your family to go on a mission trip, or signing up for the next project your church was doing for the less fortunate in your community. Success or growth in the Christian life probably looked like more and more activity that faced outward: effective evangelism, meeting needs, and activism of some sort. In short, it's all about *them and Jesus.*

Churches that fit into this category are also well and good in some ways, but *the hidden danger is that they become so focused on the external mission of God and "doing for Jesus" that they forget what it means simply to be with Him or to stop the hurry long enough to take new believers by the hand and slowly help them grow in their individual walk with God.*

organizational segmentation

Sometimes, even within a singular church, we play into the segmentation of being and doing. Think about it: on many larger church staffs, missions and discipleship (and worship for that matter) are all separate departments within the whole.

At some point it's easy for us to begin operating in silos, where we value whichever half (either being or doing) is in our area of expertise. Departmental segmentation, while not inherently bad at all, often leaks into the way our church staff and congregants view their relationship to Jesus.

If we're not careful, for example, congregants will run to the missions pastor to learn how to "do for Jesus" and run to the discipleship leaders to learn how to "be with Jesus in a quiet place." But the problem is that the missions pastor needs to be *both* a be-er *and* a do-er, and so does the discipleship leader, and so do the congregants! Life as a Christian means that every single part of the body must commit to a dual lifestyle in order for the whole church to thrive. The missions pastor will burn out—and will *model* burnout before the flock—if he only faces outward and never pulls away to be alone with God. The discipleship leader will become too insulated—and will *model* insulation—if he only prioritizes private or personal encounters with God.

All in all, the reality for any church is that outward-facing work, when not flowing from a heart rooted in a *being with Jesus*, can become activism or merely a service project with no spiritual power behind it. When we lack an abiding relationship with Jesus, our lives are automatically less fruitful. Jesus is after His people living a robust mission, but He shows us over and over again that this is to be fueled by a rich inner life with Him.

Inversely, when growing in Christ remains self-oriented and doesn't lead toward any active *doing* or engagement in God's mission, it often self-destructs. Like a stream with no place to flow, our best efforts at transformation can somehow become stagnant water in our souls, begging to flow out into a hurting and broken world.

If we happen to accidentally relegate our being or our doing in our churches to a department, a project, or a service, we can miss God's call to relate to Him in both our being *and* our doing, in a way that you can barely distinguish one from the other.

fear of extremes

As with other dichotomies, we can often camp out on one side of the "being and doing" spectrum because we are afraid of the extremes on the other side. In addition to our personality leanings or church bent, some fears could be underlying our own growth in this area.

I (Kathryn) have friends that, whenever we get together, basically have a fight over being and doing. They don't use those words, but it's at the heart of the debate every time we get together. It's comical because these friendships are decades old, and they are rich with spiritual connectivity and growth. Whenever we have the chance to go on an overnight trip or have a long conversation, though, these two friends inevitably go back to the same place, and you can see some fears and frustrations behind their words that, for each of them, originate from a holy place.

One of my friends is a be-er. She loves to be behind the scenes and has a distaste for flash. This friend is beautiful in the ways she escapes, like Jesus did, to be with her Father in solitude. She does virtuous things in secret. She writes blogs but wants her name left off. She doesn't assume that she has the best answer to the question. She's not loud in a group, but when her comments come out, they are laced with evidence of a deep walk with Jesus. We've always called her a "well." Her dad named her that because of her hidden depth. We always want more of her insight.

Another one of my friends is a gifted catalyst and leader. She is definitely more of a do-er by nature. She loves to call people up and lead them into action. She's always got a new idea for mobilizing the army of God's people, and she's full of faith that He will show up and make moves in our generation. She looks at the tremendous gifting of my be-er friend and always communicates how much she wants to help our friend *do* something with that gifting God has given her, moving it from the prayer closet out into the city streets! She develops the be-er's ideas into books and businesses and more, right before our eyes, in conversations. She believes the gifts of my *being* friend should be used in the kingdom of God in new ways, showcased for a world that could benefit and grow from her deep well of knowledge and wisdom. *What if this wasn't just about you? What if it could be used to help others grow?*

My *being* friend always resists.

My *doing* friend always pushes her.

You can hear the fears of my *being* friend come out in the conversation. She is fearful of her heart for the Lord becoming tainted. She is resistant to start doing for the sake of accolade or attention and not out of a pure heart. She wants to live the humble and quiet life Jesus modeled, not the endless rat race that is so normative in our generation. She doesn't want fame or credit. She is afraid of pride. This all stems from such a holy place.

You can hear the fears of my *doing* friend as well. She is afraid the world will miss the great depth the be-er has to offer up. She doesn't want insecurity or fear of pride to keep this gift hidden—a gift the church desperately needs right now! She wants her to reach the world with her gifting because she sees it as valuable.

She is afraid, as her friend, to see it not stewarded as God intended. This all stems from such a holy place.

In the end of this back-and-forth, they always both leave challenged because they cause each other to push back against fear and lean a little more into a fullness that God could possibly be calling them both into: *being and doing.*

integration—a vine and branches

Thankfully for us, Jesus taught about being and doing and just how necessary it is for the two to be integrated. Sometimes a single image can communicate more than a thousand words. Maybe that is why Jesus chose to use an image—a vine and branches—to help us understand the inseparable nature of being and doing.

Let's read this passage from John 15:5-8 together.

> I am the vine; you are the branches. The one who remains in me and I in him produces much fruit, because you can do nothing without me. If anyone does not remain in me, he is thrown aside like a branch and he withers. They gather them, throw them into the fire, and they are burned. If you remain in me and my words remain in you, ask whatever you want and it will be done for you. My Father is glorified by this: that you produce much fruit and prove to be my disciples.

Jesus has a way of making complex teachings simple. If we were to walk into a grape vineyard right now and observe all of the vines, branches, and fruit, it would be obvious: they are one. It would also be obvious that the fruit on the branches, though it's connected to the vine, is different from the vine itself somehow. Indeed, we'd see the fruit is the result of its connection to its source, the vine. And maybe most obvious of all, we instinctively know that if you were to cut a branch off from the vine, it would slowly wither and die. (If you've taken some grapes home from the store and thrown them in your fridge for more than a few days, you don't just have to imagine this picture; you've experienced it!) In this context and with these simple understandings, Jesus teaches about how life works with Him in His kingdom.

He states it clearly, "I am the vine; you are the branches." Jesus is the Source; we are connected to Him as living extensions of *His* being, branches. Let us not look past this too quickly. We often live our lives as if we are the source, the vine, rather than the branches. We live as if we are self-sufficient, as if we could do this on our own. I think Jesus knew this.

So He says to His disciples then, and to you and me now, *remain* in the Vine. To remain in Jesus means to learn to abide in Him. In fact, if you read this passage in multiple translations, you will find the words "remain" and "abide" used synonymously. The word in its original language is *meno*. *Meno* is a rich word with a lot of depth. Although most often translated as "remain" or "abide," another insightful definition for the word is "to continue to be present."[16] I particularly love how this definition emphasizes the ongoing connection that we are called to in Christ. Abiding isn't something we achieve; it is an ongoing way of existing in the world, a life lived in continual relationship with and dependence on Christ. To remain in Christ is to learn how to *be* with Jesus.

So, what does He say about the person who is committed to a life of *being with Jesus*? He says that the person who lives this way produces much fruit. Again, we know this instinctively—a branch connected to a healthy vine always produces fruit. Jesus says the same is true of us—when we learn to abide with Him, our lives produce fruit.

Here's another way to say it: *fruit isn't the byproduct of our greatest efforts, best strategies, or savvy leadership; rather, it is the natural and expected result of a life abiding in Christ.*

Using garden imagery, fruit doesn't exist *because* of our doing. Fruit *is* our doing; it's our offering to the world, the action born out of our connection to the vine.

Think about this. When was the last time you saw a vine or fruit tree whose fruit was luscious and attractive and yet everything else about the tree outside of the fruit was dead, stressed out, or exhausted because it was working so hard to produce fruit? You haven't. How do I know? Because the more fruit a vine or tree produces, the healthier the whole thing looks. The most fruitful trees are always the most lively, not just in the way the fruit itself looks but in total appearance. The fruit is luscious because the *whole tree* is healthy. Its roots are deep and watered. The soil around it is fertile and full of nutrients. The sunlight shines down often. The fruit looks like it's in good condition because *the tree* is in good condition. The tree has just been soaking in the right environment for many hours over the course of its life, and fruit just . . . comes out of that.

That's just how it works in nature. And isn't this opposite of how we are used to working? We tend to focus on the fruit first and worry about the tree later. We'll get to "soaking in the right environment" some other time, or if we do try to value it because we feel guilty if we neglect it, we'll try to hurry that process along so God is appeased and so we can get to the stuff that really matters. After all, our ministry stuff isn't going to run itself! And so we inevitably put accomplishment and results first and hope we have enough time and energy left over to maintain a healthy life. Yet Jesus is teaching us to do the opposite, to prioritize *being* with Him so that our *doing* is a natural and guaranteed result of our connection to Him, the Source.

So, what happens if we don't learn to *be with Jesus*?

In His next statement, Jesus gives us an answer, "If anyone does not remain in me, he is thrown aside like a branch and he withers." Jesus tells us exactly what we would expect to happen to a branch that is detached from the vine—it withers. To wither is to struggle, to decay, to progress toward death instead of life.

Have you ever felt that way—like you're withering? Just withering away with all the toil and spinning you do? Like some decent stuff is coming out of your life, but the tree itself is dry and brittle and barely making it? Trees in God's kingdom don't have to be this way. Withering is not the way of a disciple; it's the way of the world. And Jesus's teaching shows us exactly how to be vibrant again.

In the kingdom of God, a genuine piece of fruit, or an outward and active display of our faith, is *only* possible when we are tethered deeply to Jesus. When we abide. We might do important things in this life . . . sure. We could start things, we could write things, we could build things, we could get the promotion, we could find the spouse or the house, we could receive good metrics in our ministry, we could pull out all our best strategies to get that girl discipled or that lost neighbor saved, we could finally get the kids launched out into the world with a decent head on their shoulders by age eighteen, but none of this will be *kingdom* fruit if it doesn't originate from the vine. And in the end God knows the difference.

The biblical principle for us to take away here is this: our being *must* precede our doing to be effective for the kingdom.

On the other hand, a living branch can't just refuse to grow fruit any more than a woman in the delivery room can stop a baby from being born when it is time. There must always be an outward-facing action in the world resulting from our abiding relationship to the Father. When our fruit originates from *being with God*, we don't have to worry about it seeming prideful or showy because it comes from Him. It is *His* fruit, flowing through *His* branches, our submitted lives. This is a no-brainer for Jesus—which is why He makes such a fuss in the Gospels about not only *receiving* His nourishing word but *doing* it. For Him there is no way to separate such things. If we *are*, we'll *do*. If we abide in a healthy tree, *which* Jesus *is*, there's no possible way for our lives to remain barren of good works done in His name. A fruitless Christian, for Jesus, is an oxymoron. For His Father's good pleasure is to be a vinedresser who oversees a fruitful vineyard, His people, including you and me.

We should feel some sense of amazement by this. We should put it on display, not because we are amazing "fruit growers" but because the fruit in our lives is evidence of being tethered to the vine. This reveals the goodness of an amazing God who is ready to work in the lives of all of His people. Our God is a grower. He will always lean toward making us fruitful if we stay connected to Him. Isn't that something?

In conclusion, we, the branches, must learn to live in an ongoing connection to the vine, and that connection will inevitably bear fruit. We must learn to be with Jesus so that He can truly sustain and empower us to bear fruit that has a true and lasting impact in His kingdom.

Jesus was a be-er

As trustworthy teachers do, Jesus perfectly embodies His own teachings. He, after all, knows exactly what it looks like to live as a human being was intended to live. If you have ever read through any of the four Gospel accounts (Matthew, Mark, Luke, and John), you might have noticed a pattern of both being and doing in Jesus's life. A short summary of this pattern would be that Jesus regularly retreated to secluded places to be with the Father in prayer and then returned to the crowds to teach and minister to people.

Let's look closer at this pattern now, beginning with Jesus's pattern of getting away to be with His Father. Luke, in his Gospel, summarizes this aspect of Jesus's life and ministry well by simply stating, "Jesus often withdrew to lonely places and prayed" (Luke 5:16 NIV). If you search through the New Testament, you'll find more than thirty accounts of Jesus intentionally withdrawing and spending time in prayer with the Father. The pattern Luke is summarizing is evident and something the biblical writers want us to note. Jesus, carrying the greatest mission and responsibility any human being has ever carried on earth, intentionally withdraws to "lonely places."

If you're like me, I would expect the opposite. I would expect Jesus, seeing the overwhelming need in the world around Him, to squeeze every single second out of every single day, stopping for nothing other than the necessities of food and sleep to accomplish the goal set before Him. After all, that would be a noble way to live a life, wouldn't it? I doubt anyone would fault Jesus for exhausting Himself to save the world.

Yet this isn't how Jesus lived His life, and the biblical writers are trying to help us see it. Instead, Jesus often withdrew. In the face of the needs of the world, He chose to get away to a quiet place.

But why? We can rightfully assume it is because Jesus knew exactly what it would take to live a life of complete obedience to the Father. As a human, He knew that He had human limitations. He got tired, He got hungry, he needed strength that would only come through His relationship with the Father and the Holy Spirit. When Luke says that Jesus withdrew to "lonely places," he means that Jesus went to a quiet place where He could be in prayer, uninterrupted. A solitary place, a place where He could be.

Jesus's own decision to create margin in His life—to escape the constant needs of the crowds, to abide with the Father—reveals to us what it looks like to live in continual dependence on the Father and in the guidance of the Holy Spirit. In the Scriptures we see Jesus intentionally get away prior to major events in His life. He spent time *being* before He began His ministry, before He made important decisions, before He performed miracles, when He needed to deal with grief, and prior to dying on the cross.

Just watch how He handles the moments before He locks eyes with the face of His betrayer, the face of Pilate, and the cross itself:

> He went out and made his way **as usual** to the Mount of Olives, and the disciples followed him. When he reached the place, he told them, "Pray that you may not fall into temptation." Then he withdrew from them about a stone's throw, **knelt down, and began to pray,** "Father, if you are willing, take this cup away from me—nevertheless, not my will, but yours, be done."
>
> Then an angel from heaven appeared to him, strengthening him. Being in anguish, he prayed more fervently, and his sweat became like drops of blood falling to the ground. **When he got up from prayer and came to the disciples, he found them sleeping, exhausted from their grief. "Why are you sleeping?" he asked them. "Get up and pray,** so that you won't fall into temptation." (Luke 22:39-46, emphasis added)

Again, we'd expect something else here from Jesus, wouldn't we? A strategy session, perhaps. A big pep talk. A quick refresher on all the Scriptures had promised would happen so that the disciples don't act a fool when the troops come to arrest Jesus.

Yet none of that is how He handles the situation. He goes—"as usual," the passage says—to a quiet place to pray. This was His habit. This is what He always did when hard things were about to come His way. And so He kneels. He prays in anguish up to heaven, and down comes the strength He needs for what He's about to face.

And what does He expect from His disciples all this time? To do the same—to pull away and pray. And yet He finds them asleep. Shaking them from their slumber, He does not say, "Get up and make a game plan already. Judas is on our heels!" Instead He says, "Get up and pray." *That's* how He prepares for His crucifixion. He chose to pull away and *be* with His Father, the only true source of comfort or help for a task the size of the cross.

Jesus's profound works were preceded by wilderness—by desolate places. His demonstrations of strength followed His moments in silence. His life as the Savior was rooted in quiet prayer with His Father. Jesus's *being* did not compete with his *doing*. His *being* **empowered** His *doing.* And it can empower yours. In fact, He expects it to. "Get up, pull away, and *be* with your Father," He says to you and me. Will we follow His example? Or will He find us asleep?

Jesus was a doer

Can you imagine how it might feel to carry the greatest mission on earth and to realize that your path of obedience would include a rugged cross? The weight Jesus carried would have been enough to crush any one of us, yet, as we read about His life on the pages of Scripture, we see Him gracefully live the most purposeful and missional life ever lived.

As we saw in the previous section, Jesus fought for time alone, in the quiet, with His Father. He regularly withdrew to solitary places to just *be.* However, His restful and prayerful life must never be interpreted as lazy or wasteful; it was anything but that. Rather, the powerful and dynamic life Jesus lived, which drew crowds of people by the hundreds, was the outward expression of the hidden life He lived in quiet solitary moments with His Father. Jesus was fierce in His dedication to the mission the Father had for Him.

Leading into the final week before Jesus's crucifixion, commonly known as Passion Week, Luke tells us that Jesus "set his face to go to Jerusalem" (Luke 9:51 ESV). This phrase, "set his face," is an intentional phrase Luke uses to emphasize Jesus's courage and determination as He walked toward His sacrificial death. Luke wants us to know this was not happenstance. The cross wasn't just a rough situation for an unlucky guy in human history. Jesus *set His face* to do this. He meant to. He chose to. As Hebrews says, for *the joy set before Him*, "He endured the cross" (12:2). Jesus lived His entire life and ministry with this same determination. He performed miracles, taught with authority, and poured His life out as an offering unlike anyone. He was an effective missionary, a history-making movement leader, and a catalytic influencer like the world had never seen.

Where some of the Gospel accounts give us more eyes to see the "being" moments in Jesus's life, the Gospel of Mark especially gives us the sense of what His "doing" was like. If you've ever read through it, the story goes so intensely and so fast. It is an action-packed account, one scene cutting into the next, taking you through Jesus's work at lightning speed.

The pace feels like this: Jesus was *here*; then He immediately went *there*; and then while He was on His way to *this other place*, He got interrupted by *these* people; and while He was healing *them*, He chose to do *this new extra thing too*; and then *immediately* He made His way across to *this* place, and so on.

Jesus was *everywhere*, it feels like. Immediately here and then strapping on His sandals to go over there, people always crowding Him with new needs and pressing in at every turn. He was no cubicle pastor, taking a long lunch with his old college buddies and getting to the emails when He felt like it. No, Mark leaves us no room for question. When it comes to outward-facing ministry, Jesus was *doing* . . . a lot.

And yet, as we learned before, all of it was rooted in and sustained by deep communion with God. Jesus's *being* fueled His *doing*. In a world that chooses one or the other, He was a man of both.

our struggle to *be*

We all nod along when we see Jesus *being* with His Father. And yet we so obviously struggle to *be*.

Erin Westgate, a PhD student in psychology at the University of Virginia, conducted a study trying to help the way people handle just "being." The study started with an experiment: seeing how many people might choose to administer an electric shock to themselves rather than sit alone with their thoughts in an empty room for ten to twenty minutes.

The study might have seemed outlandish to some, but the researchers were anxious to see what data they would gather from a generation that doesn't know what to do when they aren't provided constant stimulation. As they brought people into the empty space, the researchers kept their phones and watches and other devices in another room. They then led the participants into the lab and gave them the option, at any time, to press a button that would allow them to self-administer a strong electric shock.

Then they would begin the study. The researchers would guide the participants simply to sit with their own thoughts for ten to twenty minutes. They were also given the strange option to press the button, an option that held no apparent benefit other than being a distraction from sitting still in the quiet.

The researchers were astonished by the results, not really expecting many people to do something as ridiculous as shocking themselves without purpose, especially in such a short amount of time alone. Erin Westgate said, "By the end of the study, we found that about 70 percent of the men and 25 percent of the women chose to shock themselves during that twelve minutes, instead of just sitting there and entertaining themselves with their thoughts."[17]

While the researchers began this study to ask how they could make people think better, they realized that the findings forced them to ask an entirely different question. Westgate put it this way: "Now the big question is, why would someone do this? Why is it so hard to just *be*, that we're willing to turn to almost anything, it seems, to avoid it?"

And she's got a point. Why *is* it so incredibly difficult to stop doing . . . to just *be*? And if we can't *be*, what's at stake? What do we risk?

While this question seems to be a modern one, it really isn't. In 1654, philosopher Blaise Pascal pondered the same questions, and in his famous work *Pensees*, he gives an answer: "All of humanity's problems stem from man's inability to sit quietly in a room alone."[18]

In other words, *all of humanity's problems* are what's at stake.

Now, there is probably more going on underneath the surface of humanity's problems than just this one thing, but we should at least admit that Pascal was on to something.

Think about it. Why do people go drinking with their friends all the time, to the point of developing terrible drinking habits? Because they don't want to sit home alone with themselves. And for the people who do want to be home "alone," why do they binge Netflix? Because it's a way to introduce other characters in the room so as to not have to sit with themselves (or with God). Why do people stare at their phones while they wait in line? Because they don't want to be alone with their own thoughts. Why do people spout off verbal lashings on those they are frustrated with? Because they didn't take the time to pull away and ponder *why* someone else's actions made them frustrated to begin with and what might be a constructive solution.

So many of humanity's problems can be tied to our inability to sit and be—to confront what's inside. That's a pretty big risk, wouldn't you say?

an enemy of intimacy

Whether or not Pascal was right about the reasons we avoid the quiet, one thing is certainly true for all of us: our enemy wants us to avoid being alone with our Father. He's so committed to keeping us away from intimacy with Jesus that he will distract us by any means necessary.

You have to wonder if this is exactly why Jesus got away regularly to pray? After all, if we think back to Jesus's words to the disciples in the garden of Gethsemane, we'd do well to remember the second half of what He said: "Get up and pray, **so that you won't fall into temptation**" (Luke 22:46, emphasis added). He knows that intimacy with the Father provides protection from the enemy's temptation. Jesus knew what it took to remain centered in the love of the Father and the empowerment of the Holy Spirit. And Satan is not unaware of what it takes, either. He knows the intimacy and power these moments had in Jesus's life. He knows that if he can keep us from avoiding this same intimacy, he can make us feel isolated, shameful, distracted, and defeated, keeping us from living the life Jesus has for us to live.

Yet, while the enemy works day and night to distract us, Jesus is continually inviting us to come toward Him, to be with Him, to learn what it is to walk with Him.

continuous partial attention

I have often wondered if there is a direct correlation between a Christian's lack of intimacy and their lack of power. What I mean by this is: we are living in a generation that is known for being a distracted generation. Microsoft researcher Linda Stone, commenting on the effect of digital distraction, says something fascinating, exposing, and helpful—that our normal way of relating is one of "continual partial attention."[19] This phrase highlights our default mode of living, which is to give only little bits of attention to whoever or whatever is in front of us. Instead of full attention, we offer our gaze to someone or something else in fits and spurts.

You probably know what Linda is talking about (and so do I). You carry on conversations while keeping an eye on your texts. You walk in a room and pull out your phone to take a picture of the environment while you half-heartedly complement the host. You answer your child in muddled *mm-hmmms* because you're also trying to scroll through something online. You think you're doing two things at once, but really you're in neither place. Wherever you show up, you're partial, not whole.

In contrast, the psalmist David, wrote:

> One thing I ask from the LORD, this only do I seek: that
> I may dwell in the house of the LORD all the days of my
> life, to gaze on the beauty of the LORD and to seek him
> in his temple. (Ps. 27:4 NIV)

David's words are like a lighthouse, allowing us to find our way home amid a million distractions. He so clearly articulates his desire for his attention to be fixed on *one thing* all the days of his life. David wanted his life to have a singular focus. So he asked the Lord to grant him this one desire.

He prayed elsewhere, in Psalm 86, that he would not only have undivided *attention* but also that he would have an undivided *heart*. He prayed, "Give me an undivided heart, that I may fear your name" (v. 11 NIV). King David is teaching us something important: the necessity of single-minded and wholehearted devotion. This is what intimacy with Jesus produces, a mind and a heart set on Him alone.

When we think about intimacy with Jesus, we often think that the lack of intimacy results in apathy toward Him. If we do not prioritize intimacy with Him, we will grow cold, lacking love. And while that may be true, another important reality is that lack of intimacy with Jesus also results in a lack of authority in our lives. And lack of spiritual authority in our personal lives leads to a lack of God's power among God's people as a whole.

We know from the Scriptures that, as followers of Christ, we have been given a measure of Jesus's authority. No, we'll never be divine as Jesus is divine. And the power He delegates to us does not find its source in ourselves but rather in Him. And yet He delegates authority to us.

Consider how David describes the authority God gives us in Psalm 8:6–8:

> You have given [mankind] dominion over the works of
> your hands;
> you have put all things under his feet,
> all sheep and oxen, and also the beasts of the field,
> the birds of the heavens, and the fish of the sea,
> whatever passes along the paths of the seas. (ESV)

Or what about the Great Commission? Right after Jesus says He has all authority, He then deputizes us to go and make disciples in His name. Up till now, Jesus has been making disciples Himself.

But once He finishes His earthly task, He tells us that we have been granted the authority and the right to make disciples.

Or consider Paul's words in Ephesians 2: "God raised us up with Christ and seated us with him in the heavenly realms in Christ Jesus, in order that in the coming ages he might show the incomparable riches of his grace, expressed in his kindness to us in Christ Jesus" (vv. 6–7 NIV). Paul is clear here that we have been seated with Christ in the heavenly realms. And where is the seat of Christ? At the right hand of the Father (Acts 2:33; 7:55–56; Rom. 8:34; Heb. 1:3). It's a seat of authority that Jesus positionally shares with us as His coheirs—as those who will forever reign with Him one day (Rom. 8:17; 2 Tim. 2:12; Rev. 3:21). This means that, in Christ, you and I now share His status and carry the full benefits of being sons and daughters of the High King. We carry His authority on this earth.

If this is true, why don't we *experience* or *exercise* such a delegated authority? Distraction. Our distracted generation is becoming a movement of Jesus's followers who lack the intimacy that comes with "being," which leads to lack of spiritual power. After all, spiritual power is the natural fruit of spiritual authority. Do we realize that our inability to *be with Jesus* is costing us more than we realize?

The invitation is this, for each of us to return to God with the cry of David, "Lord, *one thing* I ask, *one thing* I seek, to be with You, to gaze upon Your beauty, to seek You all the days of my life!" (see Ps. 27:4). Our generation is in desperate need for God to revive our hearts— our *whole* heart set at *full* attention—to *be with Him* with no agenda other than to worship and adore Him.

our struggle to *do*

As a generation, to *be* is not our only struggle. Others of us struggle to *do*—whether that's showing up to outward-facing ministry work in our own churches or showing up for Jesus's global agenda at large, ready to do our part. And yet, for even the "be-ers" of the world, there is no such thing as just *being* with Jesus without also being *led* into participation in His divine mission. As we come to life in relationship with Him, as we blossom in His presence while in the secret place, we are also meant to *bring His presence with us* as we venture back out into both our faith communities and our world. We are made not just to enjoy His kingdom ourselves but to bring His kingdom into every space we enter.

Our spirituality should always lead to missionality.

But, if we aren't careful, we will keep our spirituality to ourselves. Some of us can become comfortable with just *being.* Why is this?

As Eugene Peterson has thoughtfully observed, "*Spirituality is always in danger of self-absorption, of becoming so intrigued with matters of the soul that God is treated as a mere accessory to my experience.*"[20]

When this happens, we become so enamored with our spiritual experience and growth that we actually begin to idolize the growth instead of God Himself. It's like standing on the beach, amazed by the ocean, the sand, and the sunlight beaming through the clouds, yet failing to recognize their Creator.

When this happens, God's people and the world He created can also escape our view. The desire to grow spiritually *myself* displaces the zeal I should have for *others* to grow spiritually—for the immature, the lost, or the broken to experience the same thing I've experienced.

As Barry Jones, author of *Dwell with God for the World*, states: "*We can live out our Christian lives in an ecclesial bubble, hermetically sealed off from the corrupt and corrupting influence of the world. We may feel better about our lives, our families and our churches, but we will have betrayed our calling in the name of personal holiness.*"[21]

We can occupy ourselves more with *getting away* from the world to "be," when really, the strengthening of a "being" experience should catapult us back *into* the world, for the sake of the world. We should love being filled up, yes, but so that we might pour out.

It's easy to understand why many escape to "be" while neglecting the call to "go and do." Once we find the beauty of being with God, there is nothing like it. There is a peace and purity that doesn't compare with anything on earth. Once we find time for solitude and growth in Him, we can realize that it forms us in a way that no amount of striving ourselves could produce. We are, however, stopping short of the fullness of life that God is offering if we keep this relationship to ourselves. To have full, abundant life at our fingertips and not share it with others is cruel—and ultimately unchristian.

While we risk all of humanity's current problems if we don't *sit and be*, it seems we risk all of humanity's ultimate demise if we don't *go and do*. This is why our being and doing must be integrated as one. If we fail to integrate one or the other, we risk true vitality in our life. Like someone who is struggling to breathe correctly, the health of the entire body is compromised—not to mention the eternal hope of those outside of it.

the inhale and exhale

As we have mentioned before, our life with Jesus is a lot like breathing. That's seen most clearly when looking at being and doing. We inhale life with Him as we abide in Jesus. We then exhale life for the sake of the world. We participate in His mission with Him.

This full inhale of an abiding life fills our lungs with a peace and power, but we can't hold it in—an equal and opposite force exhales for the sake of the world.

Inhaling.

Exhaling.

In her reflections on the Christian's relationship to the world, Jen Pollock Michel talks about this dynamic in terms of a simultaneous *and* instead of an *either/or*. She recalls Jesus prayer for us in John 17. Here are His words below:

> I have given them your word, and the world has hated them because they are not of the world, just as I am not of the world. I do not ask that you take them out of the world, but that you keep them from the evil one. They are not of the world, just as I am not of the world. Sanctify them in the truth; your word is truth. As you sent me into the world, so I have sent them into the world.... So that the world may know that you sent me and loved them even as you loved me. (John 17:14-18, 23b ESV)

Michel goes on to point out something many of us miss: that Jesus prays for us to be *unattached to* the world and sanctified in His presence ("they are not of the world;" "sanctify them in the truth"), and yet, *at the same time*, committed to the world. To stay in it instead of being taken out. And on top of merely staying in it, what Jesus wants for their relationship with the world is more: to be commissioned out toward it with divine purposes and love.

She sums it up well: "Jesus prayed for his people to be sanctified— and also sent. He prayed we would be grounded in truth—and also commissioned by love. He prayed we would reject worldliness—and also love the world for his sake."[22]

Michel is right. This is the unexpected, refreshing model Jesus has for us—to be sanctified in His presence, cleansed from worldliness and yet, from that place, also sent out with His presence for the good of the world, too.

When we experience life with God as a be-er, we might be tempted to want to stay there in that place where He sanctifies us with His presence, as we have said. We might long to be separate from the world and spend our days privately experiencing this depth of life with God. But we cannot seclude ourselves to the exclusion of a world in need. We must be sent out as Jesus was.

"As the Father has sent Me," said Jesus, "I also send you" (John 20:21). It's not an obligation or duty. It becomes a burning compulsion, a deep desire you can't shake. This love is powerful enough to envelop others beyond ourselves. Michel calls it *being "emphatically for the world"*[23] in the sense that we desperately want to know God through Christ and ultimately, one day, be renewed and redeemed. In this we unite with God in His heart for the world, co-laboring with Him and bearing the burdens of those around us.

We must learn how to breathe again, to inhale the love of Christ and to exhale that same love in the world around us.

a bad master and a better motive

It would be easy at this point to think, *Great—if I "be" more, I'll "do" more. If I make time with God, I'll be given the power and authority I need to accomplish the mission. And boy, do I need some help with that. I have a lot to get done!*

At this point we'd like to throw up a warning and encourage you to go one step deeper into your understanding of the "being-doing" integration. It is so easy to buy into this integration simply because you think it will ultimately help you accomplish more ministry tasks. If you are a do-er by nature, pay attention to your motives.

It is tempting to engage in the "being and doing" dance only so as long as it leads to greater success in your *doing*.

But if you buy into "being and doing" for this reason, know that you will stumble one step before the finish line because this approach is still operating under the wrong value system—a value system that says efficiency and achievement are king. When efficiency and achievement are king, your *being* with God will always and only serve as a means to those ends. And if that's the case—if you approach this integration only for its ability to make you more productive—then you will prove time and time again that you do not worship or serve God but rather the lesser master of efficiency.

What's needed for us to take the last step in our understanding of *being and doing* is the realization that Jesus and His kingdom require not only an adoption of certain *practices* that promote being with God but also an entire overhaul of our *value system*. We can't adopt Jesus's lifestyle successfully without also adopting His values.

So let's look for a minute at Jesus's value system. What we see valued through Jesus's teachings we also see Him demonstrate with His actual lifestyle. Both reveal that His value system has less to do with efficiency, achievement, tasks, and simply getting stuff done, and centers on His *relationship* with His Father and the people around Him. In other words, Jesus oriented His entire life around *love*. Loving God with His whole heart, mind, and strength and loving other people. If you notice, those two commands, loving God and others, beautifully express both *being and doing*, resting and working, praying and acting. When we look at Jesus's life, we see that His lifestyle and value system of love are synchronous. Eugene Peterson comments about this, saying, "*The Jesus way and the Jesus truth must be congruent. Only when the Jesus way is organically joined to the Jesus truth can we get the Jesus life.*"[24]

Peterson is expressing an important point—that our lifestyles and value systems must work together congruently if we want to live a Christlike life. We cannot adopt Jesus's patterns of living yet negate His values and way of thinking. At the same time, we cannot adopt Jesus's belief system yet live a life that fails to express those same beliefs. Rather, we must intentionally seek to live lives that adopt Jesus's way of life *and* values. When we do this, we will begin to see with greater measure the love of Jesus and the life of Jesus displayed through us.

Interestingly, as we analyze His habits, how He spent his time, and what He chose to prioritize, His life often looks inefficient. Why did He take the long route to get to that city? Why didn't He just come right out and answer the Pharisees' question? Why did He let Lazarus die before raising him from the dead? These questions and many others subtly reveal the gap between our value system and Jesus's. Apparently it was more important to Jesus to encounter the Samaritan woman at the well than it was to get to Jerusalem quickly. It seems that He also cared more about revealing truth to "those who had ears to hear" than He did to constantly prove Himself right to the religious zealots of the day. And somehow, it was better for Lazarus to die, and for Jesus to weep alongside his family and friends, than it was for Him to immediately run to the rescue and heal Lazarus before he passed. Jesus's value system was different from ours. Because of that, Jesus made different decisions than we often do.

If you and I are going to take *being and doing* seriously, we must reorient our values (and our motives) from efficiency to *love*. We must go to this integration with the hope not of getting more ministry tasks done but of loving God with our whole self and loving other people. **When we do this, our rest and abiding isn't a means to effective or efficient outward ministry. Instead, truly loving God and people made in His image is a goal in itself.**

As we saw in Jesus's life, valuing time with God and other people will often lead us to a less efficient life but to a more fulfilled life. There will be times when other people scratch their heads, wondering why we are wasting our time in worship and prayer, or helping meet the needs of our neighbors; yet I firmly believe, based on Jesus's life, we will experience more of the life of Jesus displayed in and through us if we are brave enough to wade into embodying a life of being with God and doing His mission on the earth.

inward and outward miracles

Müller could have easily neglected, in his growing vision for the orphans, the things that had fueled his relationship with God in the beginning. As he pursued a life of mission, however, he remained ruthlessly committed to a life grounded in Scripture and prayer. He acknowledged, *"Often the work of the Lord itself may be a temptation to keep us from that communion with Him which is so essential to the benefit of our own souls."*[25] He realized that if he wanted to **do** things for God and His kingdom, that he could never neglect the power of **being with God** that had informed his rich inner faith from the beginning.

This doesn't mean Müller accomplished any less. In fact, in addition to preaching three times a week over the following decades, he built five large orphan houses and cared for more than ten thousand orphans. Müller's life ended up inspiring a whole movement of people to care for orphans—at least one hundred thousand orphans were cared for in England alone during his ministry.

This is perhaps still secondary, though, to the most extraordinary result of his ministry. In the end, Müller's life is said to have inspired a whole generation to pray.

Müller didn't just lean on his rich relationship with God to help him take the leap to *start* this orphan ministry. He depended on Him to *sustain* the ministry every day of its existence. This dependence perhaps was most clear in the way he prayed for specific financial provision for the ministry.

Not having any sort of wealth, Müller needed large sums of money to care for the hundreds of children God brought his way. The challenge, however, is that he felt the Lord also convicting him not to ask people directly for money. Instead, he prayed for God's miraculous provision and published for the public his reports about the goodness of God and the answers to his prayers.

Some days it was as if God literally provided for them from hour to hour.

One day they had run out of food. Three hundred children sat waiting for their breakfast. Not wavering in his faith that God would provide, George thanked God for the breakfast they were about to eat. There was soon a knock at the door, and a baker was standing outside with a big load of bread. He said that God woke him in the night and told him to bake more bread than usual and to take it to the orphanage. There was another knock at the door, and it was the milkman. A wheel on his cart had broken outside the orphanage. Not wanting to leave the cart and go and get what he needed to fix it, he offered the milk to the orphanage that same morning. Every member of Müller's staff was blown away by the Lord's provision.

In 1938, Müller came to another point when he didn't have a penny in hand, but he had hundreds of mouths to feed.

He asked his orphanage staff if there were any needless items to sell and then led his staff in prayer at nine in the morning. By ten, at his home, his wife was given a farm worker's monthly salary to cover any needs the orphans might have. This farmer said, "I felt stirred to come and bring this and have already delayed too long." By the afternoon, a woman from London who was vacationing at a home next door to the orphan house said her daughter sent an envelope of money with her for the orphan work in the area. It was a large sum of money, enough to provide for a season.

George said,

> I burst out into loud praises and thanks the first moment I was alone, after I had received all the money. I met with my staff again this evening for prayer and praise; their hearts were more than a little cheered. All of the money had been near the orphan houses for days, and that seemed proof that it was in the beginning in the heart of God to help us; but because he delights in the prayers of his children, he had allowed us to pray so long; also to try our faith, and to make the answer so much the sweeter.[26]

No one in his family or any in the orphan homes ever were without a meal or necessities. Müller's care for orphans marked his life, but these stories of dependence on God throughout the course of his ministry stirred the souls of many in Germany. The country watched as he ended up praying in millions of dollars for the orphans while never asking anyone directly for money. No one could ignore the power of the prayers of this faith-filled man.

Later in his life, Müller said that he wouldn't have done this any other way. The reason he was so adamant about his way of provision was that his whole life—especially in the way he supported the orphans by faith and prayer without asking anyone but God for money—was consciously planned to encourage Christians, primarily, that their relationship with God was real and life altering. Müller showed that the real power was in a life of *being* with God, which feeds and informs your mission with God.

Even as he was building additional orphan houses, Müller kept the need for both being and doing at the center. He said, "I saw more clearly than ever, that the first great and primary business to which I ought to attend every day was, to have my soul happy in the Lord. The first thing to be concerned about was not how much I might serve the Lord, how I might glorify the Lord; but how I might get my soul into a happy state, and how my inner man may be nourished."[27]

The power of an integration of being and doing doesn't go unnoticed. In fact, many say Muller's faith played a role in the Great Awakening, the revival of the nineteenth century. Over and over, the people watching Müller's life in the 1800s saw that when our *doing for God* is born from a deep relationship of *being with God* the miraculous happens. And all of it bends toward *people*, toward *love*, not accomplishments. May it be so in our lives.

awakened to His presence

Stories like this aren't just for heroes of our faith like George Müller. They are also for each and every one of us.

Last year my (Kathryn's) daughter stopped saying she was a Christian. She stopped taking Communion with our family, and she was mad at the Bible and God and the church. In the past year, she had seen many Christians, and even whole churches, become tangled in politics. For what actually were some good reasons, she disassociated with the church because of the persona many of its members were carrying online and otherwise.

She was at a Christian school and kept trying to learn about the Bible, but she was highly frustrated with it. She reviewed all the prophecies that had come true in Christ to see if the stats could convince her heart to reengage. Nothing was working, but she was still in the fight.

Where she was trying to distill all the facts and prove all the things, she approached me about something I had mentioned to her months before: a silent retreat. This was something I had done for years as a way to ensure an extended time of being with God, and it has always sustained my faith. When I first mentioned it, she had zero interest, but suddenly, months later, she brought it up.

I sensed that the Spirit was lighting a flame in her heart. The two of us rented a hotel room down the street, and we had the chance to just *be with God* for an afternoon and night. She said in a text:

> I finally said, "Okay, You're real and You're good because it says so right here, so what does that mean for me?" And that's when I heard Him and felt Him. It's different than I thought. It's calming and peaceful to be in His presence. I expected it to be intimidating and sort of like something you come out of with a quickened heart rate and adrenaline. Being in God's presence is something you can't really learn. There has to be a willingness to come in front of the holy Creator of everything. But now that I've experienced His presence, He is helping me understand the Bible. . . . He's bringing things to light that never made sense before.

Jesus had been working in her heart for months before that point, but this moment marked a change in her. She sat in that lobby, with music in her ears and a journal and her Bible and enjoyed His presence, without the angst and anger she had had for the past year. I sat across the lobby doing the same. It had been a tough year watching her struggle to even say the word *Christian*, but in this moment I looked across the lobby and thanked God for something *real* in my child. It had been worth fighting for. She was awakening to His presence.

awakened to mission

It's interesting that the great commandment in the Bible (the commandment to love God with all of ourselves) comes before the Great Commission of the Bible—our call to make disciples. Our daughter said that before this moment of realizing she wanted to be with God, she couldn't imagine having an inner drive to pour into others.

She was realizing what many of us are slow to recognize in our own communities. She couldn't give away what she wasn't experiencing herself. Before she was in this stage of growth, she could have been charged to go make disciples, but I'm wondering how well that would have worked out. She says that should she have tried to multiply herself in that season, she would have just replicated more sleepy or cynical Christians. So often that is what we are doing. We are calling ourselves and others to go change the world before we have experienced the presence of God in real ways ourselves. And when we try to make disciples, we end up replicating those who don't experience Him either.

After our daughter's journey with Jesus began to be enlivened by the Spirit, and she was filled with Him for this new season, we have watched her help plan worship nights at her school, speak about her faith in front of her peers, and start leading a small group. It wasn't forced; it came naturally. She wanted to do these things.

I wonder how much relief we would experience if we didn't always put the Great Commission at the center of all our mission statements. We don't ever want to neglect making disciples and living on mission, of course, but if we are growing in our love for Jesus, enjoying His presence by simply *being with Him*, the *doing* part won't feel so difficult.

moving forward together

What could this mean for each of you, if you invite the Lord to bring greater fullness into your life through both your being and your doing? What can you expect?

first, you can expect to discover profound intimacy with God

A deeper and wider well of friendship with God is offered to you—greater than you could ever imagine—if you are willing to slow down and draw from its waters. It's a friendship strong enough to uphold you in any circumstance you might encounter. It's an intimacy of relationship unlike anything you've ever known. It's an opportunity afforded you in Christ to find your soul's deepest satisfaction in God alone. If you are willing to put down the distractions and step into a life of *being with God*, you can begin to draw from these waters.

second, you can expect to discover dynamic power

There is also equal opportunity for you to live in greater power than you have ever lived. As you abide in Christ, His Spirit fills you and promises to empower you to bear fruit in the world. The kingdom of darkness stands no chance against those who are in Christ—those who are sharing in His power, His position, and His authority. If you are willing to not only *be with God* but *be sent out* by God, your *doing* can usher in Jesus's kingdom wherever you go.

a whole life with God

Let's keep growing toward all the fullness God is offering us. When it comes to being and doing, where do you lean, and how might you grow?

if you're a doer, consider this . . .

Could one or more of these ideas expand the way you relate to God?

- Start being mindful of Christ's presence through your daily activity, learning to pause and develop a sense of being with God through-out your day. Don't just go out and do stuff so you can come back later and report to Him. Remember He goes with you.

- Consider having at least one quiet time a week where you come with no agenda, simply to sit in God's presence and be with Him.

- Consider having coffee with someone who is slower and more contemplative than you are so that you can learn from someone who relates to God differently from you.

- When confronted with a problem or need, con-sider prayer as your first choice of action.

- Take a silent retreat and ask God to help you open up in His presence.

if you're a be-er, consider this . . .

Could one or more of these steps help expand the way you relate to God?

- Consider how you can share God's work in you with one other person.

- Keep your eyes open to His work around you, and when you see Jesus working in the life of others, join Him there.

- Consider having coffee with someone who is missionally-minded so that you can learn from someone who relates to God differently from you.

- Identify some areas of insecurity that keep you from engaging the world around you from the overflow of your inner faith.

- Consider various ministries your church is committed to (ministry to the poor, ministry to women or men, ministry to kids, ministry to widows or orphans, etc.). Which of them might you join to turn your faith outward?

closing poem :: breath of God

Sourced from deep within the vine,
I breathe you in, what breath divine.
my form becomes a sacred space,
I feel the Father's slower pace.

I inhale with the greatest ease,
and His life flows inside of me.
I do not have to strive and strain,
I can be, receive again.

His air fills up my vacancies
His residence awakens me
holy air contained within,
this temple now is filled by Him.

I cannot bear my chest to rise
filled with breath from the divine
without also to feel it fall
as I exhale this life to all.

it soon begins to flow from me
it slowly moves with grace and ease.
the air I just breathed in from Him
now breeds life beyond again.

this exhale rouses me to do
it guides my feet on where to move
it shows my hands on whom to lay
it guides the watching to the Way.

please Lord while I have mine left,
fill me up with every breath.
as Your breath and mine align
would You draw them to Your life through mine?

Section 4: // Saint + Sinner

As I write these words, I (Aaron) am sitting in an ICU room at a hospital close to my home in Arkansas. It's in the early hours of the morning, and I'm at the bedside of one of my closest friends. I rushed to get here. Now it's four a.m., and I feel helpless. I'm sitting at her bedside quietly watching, praying, and waiting for the doctor to come give us a report first thing this morning. My dear friend (whom I'll leave nameless here) is in critical condition, fighting for her life in this hospital bed. A long struggle with chronic illness and the pain that comes with it, compounded by depression and loneliness, has led to this dire moment for my dear friend.

It has been one of those days—you know, the kind where in just a moment's time you're confronted with the fragility of life. These types of days have a way of making time stand still. Life snaps into focus, and we see with utmost clarity, suddenly becoming aware of what's most important, and what's not.

At this moment life is sobering. I'm not sure if my friend is going to make it.

I'm weeping.

Tears stream down my face as I wrestle with the ache and deep pain of this world. I cry out inwardly, *It's not supposed to be this way. These things aren't supposed to happen!*

I feel overwhelmed. Sadness, anger, and confusion take turns washing over me like waves breaking against a rocky shoreline.

Romans 8 quickly comes to mind: "The whole creation has been groaning together in the pains of childbirth until now. . . . We ourselves . . . groan inwardly as we wait eagerly for adoption as sons, the redemption of our bodies" (vv. 22–23 ESV). And I think, "That's exactly what this feels like—groaning."

But she is still alive and fighting, so I pray again.

> *Jesus, You love her more than any of us do.*
> *Please save her.*
> *Father, help her experience Your loving presence here in this*
> *hospital room.*
> *Spirit, will you comfort us?*
> *I ask for a miracle in Jesus's name.*

Next, Psalm 139 fills my mind. "For you formed my inward parts; you knitted me together in my mother's womb. . . . Your eyes saw my unformed substance; in your book were written, every one of them, the days that were formed for me, when as yet there was none of them" (vv. 13, 16 ESV).

I think and pray,

> *Lord, what a miracle human life is.*
> *You created each of us. You know us.*
> *You know our days here on earth.*
> *There's not a single person You do not see and love.*
> *We can trust You.*
> *I trust You.*

Needing to say it once more, helping myself really mean it, I mumble it out loud,

"I ... trust ... You ... Lord."

In the days following, I began processing my experience in the hospital room. It was more powerful than I realized at the moment. As I already mentioned, important life events often help us see with greater clarity. Although much of those days remains a blur, two things stand out clearly to me:

1. Every human life is incredibly valuable.

2. Every human life is deeply flawed.

Inside the walls of that hospital, I had a sharp realization that the hospital's existence is a testament to the explicitly Christian belief that every human life is valuable. As I watched the doctors, nurses, and other hospital staff up close, it was crystal clear that they were all carefully laboring with the common goal to help all of the patients in the hospital, including my friend. Around every corner was someone playing their part. Doctors were determining diagnoses and creating plans for treatment, nurses were administering helpful medications, technicians were running labs, and the list could go on.

All to bring life and flourishing to the patients within the hospital. Beautiful.

Whether or not they knew it, they were echoing a truth revealed in Genesis 1:31.

Genesis 1:31 is the final verse of the first chapter in Scripture. Four verses prior, God culminates the created order by making humankind in His own image (an important moment we will come back to). Then after blessing them and giving them responsibility as His image bearers, we read these beautiful and weighty words,

"And God saw everything that he had made, and behold, it was *very good*." (ESV)

We should just pause here for a moment.

In the beginning ... when things were as God originally intended them to be, He looked at everything He had made and called it *very good*.

This is our origin story. This is where we come from.

This is part of who we are.

— — —

Unfortunately, the loss of human life (or nearly losing it) can be the greatest teacher when it comes to understanding the value of human life. Holding my friend's hand—and praying that God would spare her life—helped me plunge the depths of this doctrine. I began to *know*, in a much deeper way, that my friend was created by God, special and valuable, and despite any of her shortcomings or the realities brought on by a troubled world, there is something *very good* about her.

Uniquely, as much as those few days in the hospital helped me see the incredible value of every human life, it has also broadened my understanding of just how flawed we are as human beings. In the same way the existence of hospitals affirms how valuable people are, their existence also bears witness to our brokenness and the resulting brokenness of the world we live in.

Within the walls of any hospital, you'll find evidence of our fractured world—of those who sin and have been sinned against. Sickness, disease, trauma, loss, injury from violence, self-harm—again, the list goes on. Even as I type that list, I'm reminded how often I'm shielded, or at worst avoidant, of the grim reality of the human condition. Whether I want to admit it or not, the sin and suffering we live out and experience in this world bear witness to the truth of Genesis 3:6.

As beautiful and promising as chapters 1 and 2 of Genesis are, Genesis 3, in many ways, is the complete opposite. Adam and Eve, created to live with God and flourish on earth, disobeyed God's good intention for them and ate of the fruit. Genesis 3:6 recounts this part of the story.

> So when the woman saw that the tree was good for food, and that it was a delight to the eyes, and that the tree was to be desired to make one wise, she took of its fruit and ate, and she also gave some to her husband who was with her, and he ate. (ESV)

Eating the fruit was much more serious than it might appear. Eating the fruit was blatant rebellion, a choice to distrust God and seize autonomy; it was actively choosing death instead of life. This chapter of Scripture is commonly known as the "fall of man," a decisive point in human history, a crack that penetrated and damaged every part of God's good creation. What began as a crack quickly turned into a monumental earthquake fracturing human life—and even creation's life—at every level.

The next few chapters of Genesis, chapters 3–11, go on to describe the devastating effects of sin. God repeatedly gives humanity the chance to steward His good world, and humanity consistently ruins it. We begin to see the hospital list from above emerge on the pages of Scripture. Jealousy and deceit lead to murder. Power and oppression lead to a multitude of great evils and pains. The cracks deepen, and the severity of the fall widens. Eventually, this part of the story culminates in chapter 11 at Babel, where the people have become so self-sufficient in their own eyes, so flawed in their thinking, that they seek to build a tower that reaches up to the heavens so they can "make a great name for [themselves]" (v. 4 ESV). In many ways, reading Genesis 11 is like watching a replay of Genesis 3, only the scene does not include just one person being *deceived* and then acting in rebellion and then hiding. Rather, it shows a whole group of self-absorbed, self-serving people collectively deciding, in plain sight, to defy their good and benevolent God. Humanity continues to choose autonomy rather than trust in the Creator, which leads to greater and greater destruction.

In the same way the loss of life can be our greatest teacher in valuing human life, it can also bring us face-to-face with the brokenness we've created. We live many centuries "downstream" of the events of Genesis 3–11, yet we don't have to look far to see the same story playing out in our day.

As I sat next to my friend, I *felt* these fractures at a deeper level, knowing that everything that is not right in our world somehow traces back to that day in the garden. We were made very good, but now we're very broken.

We should pause here as well. Let this sink in a bit more.

This is a part of our origin story. This is where we come from.

This is part of who we are.

saint or sinner

The pressing question in this chapter is, Are we saints or sinners? Our thinking around this subject is important because it is the lens through which we view ourselves and other people every day. We want to be clear here—we will be talking particularly about the identity of those who are saved in Christ, those who have been rescued from darkness and brought into glorious light (1 Pet. 2:9). We will go back to the beginning and look at what it means to be human—the end goal of this chapter is to discover afresh what the Bible says about being saints and sinners.

Admittedly, this is the most difficult chapter for us to write in this book. Not because we are conflicted about its message but because we are well aware that to advocate for *both/and*, when it comes to biblical tensions like we are exploring, often results in upsetting people on both sides of the discussion. This chapter in particular feels to us to be the "thinnest ice" in this book. That is mostly because the subject matter is so central to our beliefs about who we are, which has an implicit connection to the gospel message we teach and proclaim. This is also the reason we have such conviction and confidence to explore our identities as God's people.

With that said, let's get to it.

we all lean

There tends to be monumental confusion in the church when answering the question about us, as followers of Jesus, being saints or sinners.

As we have seen, we tend to separate when it comes to biblical tensions.

In some circles, we hear this language about ourselves and fellow believers:

> We are **sinners**—*filthy rags, hopeless worms in need of Jesus every single moment. There's nothing good about us but Him!*

In other circles, we hear a different statement about ourselves:

> We are **saints**—*new creations who are part of the priesthood and family of God, with His Spirit empowering us every moment. We've been made new!*

According to our bent, we probably can look at those two statements and know instantly which phrases we have identified with the most closely.

What about you? Given various external and internal forces in your life, there are likely many reasons you might identify with one of those statements more than the other.

Some of the strongest external forces are probably your personal church upbringing (if you had one) and what your parents emphasized during your formative years. When it comes to church, did you hear more sermons that made you feel like, even after salvation, your life was mostly marked by sin and depravity? Or did you hear more about victory in Christ? When it comes to your parents, did you hear more about what you were doing wrong or about all the good ways you reflect God in the world?

Our personalities can also cause us to lean toward thinking about our value or thinking about our sin. Are you a perfectionist by nature, always noticing the ways you don't measure up? Are you "easy on yourself" and confident, naturally able to laugh at your mistakes and embrace the good in yourself and in other people?

Here are some general clues that might help you discover how you lean when it comes to your identity and how you see yourself:

Saint Language	Sinner Language
I am a child of God.	There is no good in me.
I make mistakes but am approved by God.	Apart from Him I can do nothing.
I am a new creation.	I don't know why He chose me.
I am made holy.	I am nothing without Him.

There is truth in each of these statements, but I bet you've rehearsed one side of these truths far more often than the other. And you're not alone. Personality, parents, and church considered, we all end up leaning one way or the other.

different streams

As with our other dichotomies, and as we just nodded to in the previous paragraphs, the church you've been a part of heavily influences whether you see yourself as primarily sinner or saint. And as all churches are, that church in your mind's eye is part of a historical stream.

For some streams of the church, and for all sorts of historical reasons, the teaching is focused more on sin and depravity. There is a marked emphasis on your inability to do good.

That being the case, if you relate to this stream, you're probably familiar with passages like this:

> **For I know that nothing good lives in me,** that is, in my flesh. For the desire to do what is good is with me, but there is no ability to do it. (Rom. 7:18, emphasis added)

This emphasis reflects a desire to hold high the person and work of Christ by teaching the fallenness of man with weightiness. And that's not bad; it's actually an incredibly important and central truth of the Christian faith.

Simultaneously, for other streams, the teaching revolves more around our new identity in Christ. There is an emphasis on our sainthood as we are named fellow heirs of Jesus.

If this sounds familiar, you probably know your way around passages like this:

> Therefore, **if anyone is in Christ, the new creation has come**: The old has gone, the new is here! (2 Cor. 5:17 NIV, emphasis added)

Leaning our emphasis in this direction often reflects a desire to step into the new identity given to us in Christ with gratitude and power. And again, that's not bad; it is *also* an incredibly important and central truth of the Christian faith.

The problem does not lie in either of these teachings; rather the problem is when we emphasize only *one* of these truths at the expense or exclusion of the other. For various reasons, we avoid nuance and easily slip into dogmatic stances on only one side in a way Scripture doesn't.

Just as it is with other dichotomies we've explored in this book, this polarized stance of only claiming the identity of *sinner* or only recognizing our identity as *saint* can often be because of deep fears associated with "the other side."

fear of extremes

So, what fears do we carry around and even bow ourselves before? What are we so afraid of?

for starters, the fear of getting stuck in sin

Many of us quickly get uncomfortable thinking about our sin. Who wants to address it? It's painful and humbling. So in many cases, we avoid the inward search required to let God reveal the wayward parts of our hearts. We know it's there, but we don't want to face it or get stuck in a cycle of despairing over it. So we avoid looking back, confessing sin and repenting. We are sure that if we dig we will find quite a bit that brings shame and discomfort. After all, we've seen enough Christians living their entire lives in shame, held constantly lowered in despair, forever stuck in sin spirals! Who wants to be like them?

Some even live as if we have no sin left. The assumption is that because the *power* of sin is broken in our lives and we're given new hearts by God, then the *presence* of sin is now totally gone, too—that there's no sin remaining in us that needs to be weeded out. While that is true for our future with Jesus in the age to come, until He returns, we must treat sin as though it is still present within us.

Why? Because the New Testament has plenty of examples of genuine believers who need help repenting of their current sin, even though they've been saved. The book of 1 Corinthians alone has more than ten situations in which this is the case! And then there's Hebrews 12:1, which tells us we must constantly "lay aside" sin which so easily entangles and ensnares us. I could go on, but the assumption of the Bible is that sanctification is a lifelong process and that sin is still something we have to fight as believers. It's not simply "gone" on this side of eternity.

Because the presence of sin still hangs around, we ought to pursue godliness, putting off the old sinful self and putting on the new holy self. This is the exact idea the apostle Paul explains to believers when he tells them in Colossians 3:5-10 (ESV) to "put to death therefore what is earthly in you" and instead, "put on the new self" (we'll get to more on this concept soon!).

If we look closely at the language, it's clear Paul assumes there are still some "earthly" things going on with the Colossians. Pay attention to *where* they are going on. "*In* you." Paul is talking to believers with new lives and new hearts, yes, but he makes the point that sin is still *in* the human heart after conversion, and it has to be put to death on a daily basis. What kinds of earthly, sinful things, you wonder? Paul gets specific: "sexual immorality, impurity, passion, evil desire, and covetousness, which is idolatry . . . anger, wrath, malice, slander, and obscene talk from your mouth" (vv. 5, 8 ESV).

The Scriptures reveal that there is still darkness inside believers, being slowly brought into the light. In the end—whether it's because we genuinely didn't know it was there or because we did but just didn't want to look at it—any of us are more than a little fearful to address such darkness within. It can be easier to neglect confession of sin, afraid we will give it too much attention and get stuck in the "old self" (or the shame that comes with it). We're afraid of becoming like those Christians who, honestly, are either constantly in sin or just seem bummed all the time. This fear causes many of us to wrongly neglect Scripture's teaching to confess sin in order to receive healing.

> Therefore confess your sins to each other and pray for
> each other so that you may be healed. (James 5:16 NIV)

the fear of getting stuck in pride

On the other hand, some of us are just as afraid to embrace our saintly nature in Christ as doing so raises many unsettling questions. Will embracing our new identities as fellow heirs of Christ lead us to being presumptuous and prideful? Will it cause us to rely less on God's grace? Will it tempt us to stop confessing sin or avoid fighting the flesh? Will it make us one of those kinds of Christians on the other side—the ones who are haughty and irreverent?

With all these fears swirling within us, we wonder: *Who are we to call ourselves saints? Isn't that the furthest thing from humble?* A fair question. Problem is, while we may not feel as if we have the right to throw around the word *saint*, *God* has called us this. *God* is the one who insists on it! As we'll see in just a moment below, He calls us "saints" . . . *a lot*. And so it seems that sometimes in an attempt to embody humility, we dismiss much of the new reality that God *insists* is true about us: that we are now saints, priests, brothers, sisters, holy sons and daughters made righteous in Christ.

It may feel easier for some of us to solely claim the identity of "sinner" so that we don't become prideful and arrogant. In doing so, however, we err from truth by not receiving our new identities found in Christ—by disagreeing with God Himself on *who He says we are* in Him. *Beloved, chosen, washed, redeemed* . . . the list goes on. The Bible will never open up to bestow some other set of words when it comes to who the church is. These are the words God has chosen to use when He speaks about our identity in the New Testament.

See, similar to how avoiding the *sin* part of our nature keeps us from experiencing the healing God wants to give us, avoiding the *saint* part of our nature keeps us from experiencing the honor He wants to give us.

And yet, out of our fears, we lean further and further into one side or the other, don't we? We resist the both-and. We think: *Maybe camping out here is much easier.*

It may be easier, friend, but it's not full. By living in the fear of whatever extreme you're afraid of, you miss out on the fullness of all God says about *who you are.*

So, how do we get the fullness? Well, in order to explore this more, we need to go back to the beginning of our stories. We can learn a lot about ourselves and about redemption in Christ by understanding where we came from.

origin story

I (Aaron) was recently getting my hair cut by a new barber. As he invited me over to his station in the barbershop, wondering what kind of haircut I was about to get, I began to notice a few things about him. He was young, had darker skin, long curly hair, trendy black attire, and a cool accent, which revealed that English was not his first language. So naturally, I asked him, "Where are you from?"

"Colombia," he said.

That one question and answer fueled our conversation for my entire haircut. "Where are you from?" ultimately led to "So, how'd you get here?" And eventually, "Where are you wanting to go?" I was fascinated hearing his story.

As David told me bits and pieces about his life in broken English, I learned about who he is as a person. What's true about David is true about all of us: where we come from and our place of origin shapes us. It's an undeniable part of who we are.

This is one of the reasons the book of Genesis is so important to our discussion in this section and why we're about to go back and explore it at a greater depth than we have already. Genesis brilliantly introduces a number of the most central themes of the Bible, all in the first few pages of the story.

In particular, we quickly gain a picture of who God is—the eternal Creator, and who we are—created beings. However, we also see that God is not the only being in the garden of Eden with an agenda. We are also introduced to His enemy, Satan, the serpent. Shortly following the serpent's introduction, as we have already seen, the fundamental problem enters the story: human sin and its enslaving power.

origins of our identity

Let's pause for just a moment and ask a helpful question. Based on what we see in the origin story of Genesis chapters 1–3, what would you say is inherently true about human beings after the fall?

Is worth embedded in every human?

Is sin embedded in every human?

The answer, from a biblical perspective, is ... yes.

Both are true.

Now, I know, depending on your background and what you might have grown up believing about humanity, there's a good chance this answer might feel like a stretch to you. That's exactly why we need to dive deeper.

From a theological viewpoint, we are now discussing the biblical tension between two important Christian beliefs: *human dignity and human depravity*. Hang with us here because these two beliefs are directly connected to our discussion around saints and sinners and will be helpful for us moving forward.

Let's unpack this concept. Here is what these two ideas mean:

Human dignity describes the inherent value and worth of every life.

This concept is introduced in Genesis 1:26 (NIV) where God says, "Let us make mankind in our image, in our likeness." A mentor of ours, theology professor at Western Seminary, Dr. Gerry Breshears, refers to human dignity as our *first Adamic heritage*. What Gerry means by that is that through Adam, the first man, every human being has inherited dignity because we are all created in the image of God. The point is that just as our forefather Adam and foremother Eve were designed with God's image embedded inside them, so it is for every person born under and after them—including you and me. They passed this dignity down to us. We see this idea of all humans being made in God's image carried throughout the Scriptures, oftentimes brought up when humans are being treated wrongfully.

One example of this is when James writes about the importance of taming the tongue. He says that with the same tongue we "praise our Lord and Father, and with it we curse human beings, who have been *made in God's likeness*" (James 3:9 NIV, emphasis added). In other words, the whole reason we should never curse another person, James says, is because human beings bear God's image. *God* made them. They inherited dignity from Adam and Eve just as you and I did. And so to insult them is to insult the Maker who crafted them in His own likeness. If you have a problem with a person, then you have a problem with someone who has a strong resemblance to God Himself! *That's* why humans have innate worth, no matter who they are.

Human depravity, on the other hand, describes our inherited human sinfulness and alienation from God due to that sin.

This concept is introduced in Genesis 3:1-24, but becomes even clearer in passages such as:

- Psalm 14:2-3, which shows us that "the LORD looks down from heaven on the entire human race; he looks to see if anyone is truly wise, if anyone seeks God. But no, all have turned away; all have become corrupt. No one does good, not a single one!" (NLT).

- Or Romans 5:12 which says, "Therefore, just as sin entered the world through one man, and death through sin, and in this way death came to all people, because all sinned" (NIV).

Dr. Breshears refers to this passage in Romans as our *second Adamic heritage*. In the same way we all inherited dignity as members of the human race, we have also inherited depravity, a broken and sinful nature. Said another way, our forefather and our foremother passed down both the good *and* the bad.

Although these two truths might seem like they contradict each other, they actually work together.

Both are true.

Both are necessary to our understanding of who we are.

Both hold space with each other throughout the entirety of the Bible's story.

Both tell the truth about our origin story, and both give a satisfying explanation for why you (and the whole world, really), are somehow simultaneously capable of doing both beautiful and bonehead things.

Human dignity reveals the inherent worth of humans without denying the reality of their sinfulness.

And human depravity offers a reason for why they are flawed and corrupt in the first place, lost and separated from God, all without denying their value.

hold the tension

As we have seen throughout this book, it is a struggle for us to hold tension as well as the biblical writers do, and the tension between *sinner* and *saint* is no different. On one end, we often feel like we can't say anything good about someone else because we remember that "no one is good" (Rom. 3:10). Or, on the other end, we feel like we can't be honest about sin because we don't want to talk negatively about those who are "fearfully and wonderfully made" (Ps. 139:14 ESV).

So instead of learning to hold the tension, we let go and subsequently fall on one side or the other.

In doing so, however, we slowly move away from not only the fullness of who we actually are but also away from biblical faithfulness.

beautiful yet bankrupt

Yet Scripture won't let us give up that easily. It tries to teach us how to walk the line in a healthy way and invites us into a fuller perspective than we'd usually allow ourselves. To correct those who view human beings as nothing but cosmic garbage, it reveals that all human beings—both the saved and the unsaved—have the fingerprints of God on them. They bear His image in a way that shows an innate beauty that mirrors the Creator.

> *Your neighbor.*
>
> *The garbage man.*
>
> *A child too young to speak and fully understand the gospel.*
>
> *The store owner.*
>
> *A guy on a motorcycle next to you on the highway.*

That person or group of people online you're always tempted to lash out against.

Our hearts should burn with love for the people God so intentionally created. They carry an inherent goodness. We can hear God's words echoing in our ears and agree with them as we encounter humans of every color, any creed, either gender, and all nationalities. God saw all that He had made, and it was very good indeed (Gen. 1:31).

God sees them as masterpieces He created and loves.

Also, in the same breath, Scripture corrects those who deem humans "perfect just as they are," helping them remember that every human being is fatally flawed and in need of the saving grace of Jesus. While we bear God's image, we bear it in brokenness. The image of our Creator still remains, but it is a dim reflection of what once was. Like a shattered mirror, we look at ourselves, and we see what God's image was *sort of supposed to* look like, but things are fractured and marred. It's clear the reflection doesn't tell the whole story of exactly what it should. This brokenness has alienated us from our relationship with God, enslaved us to sin and death, and left us utterly reliant on God for both our spiritual and physical rescue.

When we take in the full counsel of Scripture and let it adjust our perspective, we'll see that every person around us, although inherently valuable, also carries an immeasurable need for salvation. We'll see that we are valuable yet needy. Wonderfully made yet terribly marred. Beautiful yet bankrupt.

an incomplete story

Taking the time to go back to our beginnings can help us understand who we are *apart* from Christ. Specifically, we are complex. We are both made in God's image, carrying goodness and dignity everywhere we go, and also fallen and rebellious creatures, carrying brokenness and depravity into everything we are.

We have taken this journey because understanding who we are prior to knowing Jesus directly correlates to our understanding of who we are after we have received salvation in Christ. However, that correlation might be different than you would think.

It is pretty easy to see the connection between being a sinner and our inherent depravity (sinfulness). The same sin that broke the world, enslaved us, and left us in desperate need of God's grace is the same sin we still wrestle with for all of our lives (albeit, because of Christ, we are no longer enslaved by its power as we once were). Put differently, we are considered sinners in this life precisely *because* we're inherently depraved.

But what about the connection between "saint" and our inherent human dignity? Are we considered saints in this life *because* we're inherently dignified? No—in fact, there is a huge distinction to be seen here. The distinction is this: while every human being carries God-given dignity, *only* those who are saved in Christ are given the ultimate title *saints*, holy and beloved children brought into the family of God. Stated another way, apart from Christ we carry the dignity of being made in God's image, but we remain irreparably broken, flawed, and fragmented, *without the hope of being restored and redeemed*. While it's beautiful to recognize dignity, it's still horrible to live a life without the possibility of restoration. And even worse, to die without receiving salvation.

This is how our origin story correlates so powerfully to our new life in Christ. In Jesus there is invitation to *both*, to be saved from our sin *and* restored to bear God's image more and more clearly for the rest of our lives.

Let's look at this a different way so that we can see the beauty of the gospel message with even more brilliance.

Growing up, the most common explanation of the gospel, the good news of the story of Jesus, that I heard went something like this:

> We are all sinful and have fallen short of God's glory. Therefore, we are separated from a holy God and need a perfect substitute to die in our place so that our sins can be forgiven. The good news is that Jesus came to earth, lived a sinless life, and died on a cross in our place. Now we must confess our sins and believe in Him, and we will receive salvation.

I (Aaron) would guess that many of you have grown up hearing some form of that same message. If you are in that category like I am, we ought to have a profound thankfulness to have grown up hearing about salvation that is found in Christ alone. Not everyone has had that wonderful privilege.

With that said, as I have journeyed with Christ, like many of you, I have run into my own roadblocks along the path. When I say roadblocks, I mean dry seasons, lack of growth, and questions that need answering along the way. As I have sought answers and wrestled my way through such seasons, I have realized some of those roadblocks are because I had only a partial understanding of the story rather than a whole one.

For me, there were aspects to the story of God that I was, quite frankly, completely missing out on. The gospel message I grew up with was a wonderful place to begin but failed to give me an understanding of the fullness of redemption in Christ. And because of that, my mental picture of "life in Christ" had some major gaps that hindered my spiritual growth.

Here is what I mean by that: the Bible, as a whole, is a unified story that leads to Jesus (a definition borrowed from our friends at The Bible Project). Therefore, it's essential that we see the *entire narrative* as crucial context for understanding the gospel message. When we look at it closely, the story is often divided into four acts:

CREATION > THE FALL > REDEMPTION > RESTORATION

Now I want you to notice how the gospel message I grew up with, the one stated above, leaves out any trace of two important parts of the story: the creation and then the restoration. We leave off the bookends.

Instead, notice that my gospel narrative began with **"we have all sinned and fallen short of God's glory."**

Unknowingly, I was completely ignoring Genesis 1–2 and the importance of the creation narrative and its themes that play out in the overall story.

Also notice that my gospel narrative ends with redemption and leaves out restoration.

"Now we must confess our sins and believe in Him, and we will receive salvation."

I was rightfully taught about redemption in Christ, particularly the forgiveness of sins, but again, unknowingly leaving out the last movement of the story, where many of the main biblical themes find their resolution.

Instead of the four acts above, the visual representation of my two-act gospel narrative would have looked something like this:

THE FALL > REDEMPTION

I've realized my partial understanding of the biblical story is that what I received when I came into the faith was not **inaccurate** at all, but it was **incomplete** for a full understanding of what Jesus accomplished on my behalf and what that means for my new life in Him.

Practically speaking, I could only identify with what it meant to be a sinner. To consider myself a saint felt ludicrous. I could only see my failure, my brokenness, my depravity. *I'm fallen! I'm weak! I'm hopeless!* And because of that, I was exhausting myself to try to live up to some unattainable standard I hoped would earn God's favor in my life. I had little to no understanding of my worth in God's eyes or how He wanted to restore to me all that was lost.

So I want to share with you a few important themes, each intro-duced in the creation story, that weave their way throughout the entire narrative arc of the Bible. They end up playing an important role in how we see ourselves as God's people.

creation themes

- The creation narrative introduces human beings as part of God's good creation who bear His image.
- Humans were created to live in relationship with God forever.
- Humans were created to partner with God and to co-rule the world He created with Him.

This is huge! Don't miss God's original heart and intention toward humanity. This is what I missed for so many years. *God's heart was for relationship and partnership with us from the beginning.* God val-ued His creation and *wanted* to be with us. And because I missed this, I spent *years* of my life believing God was primarily and perpetually mad at me, disappointed in me, annoyed that He had to be near an earthling like me, and waiting on me to get my act together.

Now watch what happens to these themes when sin and its enslaving power are introduced to the story line.

effects from the fall

- After the fall, each of us still carry the image of God, but that image is greatly marred by sin.

- After the fall we are relationally separated from God and enslaved to sin, unable to conquer its power.

- After the fall we are no longer suitable to partner with God. Instead we have become His enemies.

This is what I missed here—pay attention—*God's heart was and is grieved by the fall.* Without an understanding of God's heart for creation, we don't see the pain our sin and rebellion caused God. It grieved His heart when His creation turned against His perfect rule and reign.

You may be thinking, *But does God also have righteous anger toward us for our full-out rebellion?* Absolutely. But His holy anger is rooted in love for His children, which is why we see Him repeatedly moving back toward relationship with us, mediating His presence in various ways throughout Scripture. What does this mean? It means *He wants to be near earthlings like us—an earthling like you.* Eventually, to pull this off permanently, God's love and presence were perfectly mediated to us through Jesus, "the image of the invisible God" (Col. 1:15). God came to us, His presence wanting to come so near that He *walked among us* in the person of Christ. So let's see how these themes play out further.

redemption in Christ

- In Christ, God is "recreating" us and restoring His image in us. He's mending the shattered mirror so we can look like we were always meant to look.

- In Christ, our relationship to God is restored and renewed, the power of sin is broken, and the Holy Spirit is given to us. Not only did God's presence walk *among* people in Christ two thousand years ago, but His presence now resides *inside* people through His Spirit who indwells believers. We become God's dwelling place.

- In Christ, we receive a new identity, we are no longer known by our mistakes or sin's enslaving power. We are now saints of God, redeemed to partner with God on His mission in the world.

Again, this is what I missed for so long—the themes from Genesis 1–2 are now picked back up and recovered in the gospel! Because I had an incomplete view of the Bible's story, I only knew that I was sinful and separated from God; therefore, I saw forgiveness and atonement for sin as the *only* aspects of redemption in Christ. I never noticed that God was also redeeming His image in me and reinstating me to co-labor with Him in the world! Dwelling in me, being near me—this wasn't something that annoyed Him. *It's what He wanted all along with humans!* To dwell with them, to rule and reign next to them!

Now please hear me. I do not mean to underplay the astonishing importance of the forgiveness of sin in any way. I'm just saying, "Can you believe it—there's even more!"

When you begin to see a fuller picture of what God has accomplished for you in Christ, you will also begin to understand your new identity as a saint, one of God's holy people. Sin is a huge part of our story—there's no doubting that—but it no longer defines who we are.

This reality becomes even clearer as we look into the next movement of the story, *restoration*.

These themes play out from the moment of salvation throughout our eternal future.

restoration of all things

- In Christ, we are now being increasingly transformed into His likeness through the power of the Holy Spirit every day, a process called *sanctification*. One day we will end that process and enjoy a new one where we're fully redeemed and dressed in radiantly resurrected bodies, something called *glorification*.

- In Christ, friendship with God is now available, and we will one day dwell with Him forever in the new creation. That's right—His renewing power is not only for humans; it's for the whole world. One day the curse of sin and decay will be lifted from the entire earth.

- In Christ, saints now co-labor in His kingdom, and we will co-rule and reign with Him in the new heavens and new earth for eternity.

Again, mind blown! The same themes are ringing throughout the entire story line of the Bible that I had somehow missed for years of my life following Jesus.

As it relates to being saints and sinners, if I had to summarize in one sentence what I missed all of those years, it would be this:

> Sin defiled God's people, but in Christ it does not define them.

Now let's take a look at one specific New Testament passage and see how Paul addresses this exact idea.

made alive in christ

Ephesians 2:1–10 is a passage that brings the concept of sinner and saint together more than any other. Read these verses and listen to how the apostle Paul speaks both about sin and the new identities of those who are in Christ.

> And you **were** dead in your trespasses and sins in which **you previously walked** according to the ways of this world, according to the ruler of the power of the air, the spirit now working in the disobedient. We too all **previously lived** among them in our fleshly desires, carrying out the inclinations of our flesh and thoughts, and we **were** by nature children under wrath as the others were also. But God, who is rich in mercy, because of his great love that he had for us, **made us alive** with Christ even though we were dead in trespasses. You are saved by grace! He also **raised us up** with him and seated us with him in the heavens in Christ Jesus, so that in the coming ages he might display the immeasurable riches of his grace through his kindness to us in Christ Jesus. For you **are** saved by grace through faith, and this is not from yourselves; it is God's gift— not from works, so that no one can boast. For we **are** his workmanship, created in Christ Jesus for good works, which God prepared ahead of time for us to do. (emphasis added)

Wow, what a beautiful passage.

First, let's look at how Paul talks to the church in Ephesus about sin and their relationship to it. He says . . .

1. They were dead in their trespasses and sins. In other words, their sinful nature, sinful choices, and intentional wrongdoing made them not just "bad" people, but also led to a state of spiritual deadness. They weren't sick. They weren't "almost there" in their spiritual journey, just needing an extra pep talk from Jesus. No. They were *dead* in their sins. And dead people can't reach up out of the coffin and save themselves. Spiritually speaking, before coming to Christ, we were dead men walking.

2. They were following the ways of this world and the ruler of the kingdom of the air, and therefore under God's wrath. Contrasted against following the ways of God and living under His good reign, Paul reminds the church in Ephesus that at one time in their history, they had chosen, instead, to follow the ways of the enemy and the world. Because of their deadness in sin and their followership of the enemy, they were understandably under God's wrath.

Notice something important again: Paul refers to all of this in the *past tense*. He says, "You *were* dead in your transgressions and sins, in which you *previously* walked." Paul even says, "We too," meaning the apostles, "*previously* lived" according to the ways of the world. The apostles, too, along with the other believers in their past life, "were" under God's wrath.

But then something happens.

3. They are now alive with Christ and have therefore been given a new and different identity. Suddenly, in verse 5, Paul shifts from what was *previously* true to what is *now* true for those in Christ. Do you see it? He says:

- We are alive in Christ.
- We are seated us with Him in the heavenly realms.
- We are God's workmanship.

Do you see it? Instead of saying that these Ephesian believers don't sin anymore, Paul is emphasizing a major identity shift that has occurred in the life of each person who is now *alive in Christ.*

Look at the contrast Paul makes between verses 1-3 and verses 4-10.

> We *were* dead. Now we are *alive with Christ!*
>
> We *used* to be slaves to sin. Now we are *seated with Christ* in the heavenlies!
>
> We were *deserving* of wrath. Now we have received salvation *by grace, through faith!*

At the risk of repeating myself, I'm going to say it a different way. Of course the Ephesian believers *were* dead in their trespasses and sins, *but that is no longer their identity.* They are now ALIVE WITH CHRIST! Of course the Ephesian believers will wrestle with sin in the days to come, but they are *no longer defined by it*, and it is now no longer a "given" that they will walk in it; they have been given a new identity.

And as the summary statement for this entire section, Paul writes, "We are his workmanship, created in Christ Jesus for good works, which God prepared ahead of time for us to do.

Pay attention here, this is so important.

In the original language, the word "workmanship" is *poiema*, and can also be translated as "handiwork" or "poem." The word *poiema* is, uniquely, used in only one other place in the entire New Testament, where it refers specifically to the act of the first creation (back to Genesis again!).

This is so important because it helps us see that Paul is making an intentional connection between the original creation and the salvation of the believers in Ephesus. Just as in the beginning, there is an act of God creating anew.

In Genesis, humanity was created by God, and now, because that original creation was ruined or "de-created" by sin, God has *re*-created us, recovering that which He originally made!

Paul writes with similar emphasis in 2 Corinthians 5:17 when he says, "Therefore, if anyone is in Christ, **the new creation has come: The old has gone, the new is here**!" (NIV, emphasis added).

Paul takes us back to the beginning to help us understand our new identity in Christ. As we choose to follow Him, we're no longer defined by our sin, enslaved by its power, or identified as *sinners*. We are now *new creations*, sons and daughters of God, saints. This is who we are.

Is sin a part of the Ephesians' story? Absolutely. Will it forever be a part of their lives this side of the new creation? Yes, it will. But it is no longer *who they are*.

Now, look again at the words Paul uses for these believers in verse 1 of the book. He writes to the Ephesians: "To God's holy people in Ephesus, the faithful in Christ Jesus" (NIV).

Notice he doesn't say, "To God's sinners in Ephesus." No. Look again.

Those who were faithless are now called "faithful in Christ."

Those who were dead and enslaved to sin are now named as God's *living*, "holy people."

Those who were undoubtedly identified as sinners are now saints.

This is the beauty and power of the gospel.

the sinner in Scripture

Still, in many of our circles, we hear Christ followers make this statement around their own identity:

"Me? I'm just a sinner saved by grace!"

While I understand why people say this, in light of the whole biblical story, we must question if this is an accurate statement about who we are as believers.

In Romans 5, particularly in verses 6 and 8, we read words, again, that might have influenced our descriptions of our identities:

You see, at just the right time, when we were still powerless, Christ died for the ungodly.... But God demonstrates his own love for us in this: while we were still sinners, Christ died for us. (NIV)

Upon first glance, these verses seem to confirm the fact that we are indeed, as believers, sinners saved by grace. After looking more closely, though, we see again that the past tense is used—"while we were still sinners." This phrase seems to highlight, as we also saw in Paul's letter to the Ephesians, a past identity, different from the present identity Paul uses to describe his fellow believers in the rest of his letters. In fact, at the beginning of Romans, Paul made the identity of his brothers and sisters clear as he addressed them "to all those in Rome who are loved by God and called to be *saints* (Rom. 1:7 ESV, emphasis added). Paul could have chosen to address his letters to "sinners," but he clearly does not. He repeatedly refers to God's people, those who have come to a saving faith in Jesus, according to their new identity as "saints" of God.

Let's look at a couple more examples. Take a look at these verses about sinners and consider, in what context is the term being used—as a designation for those who don't know Jesus or for those who do?

> On hearing this, Jesus said, "It is not the healthy who need a doctor, but the sick. But go and learn what this means: 'I desire mercy, not sacrifice.' For I have not come to call the righteous, but **sinners**." (Matt. 9:12–13 NIV, emphasis added)

> If you love those who love you, what credit is that to you? Even **sinners** love those who love them. And if you do good to those who are good to you, what credit is that to you? Even **sinners** do that. And if you lend to those from whom you expect repayment, what credit is that to you? Even **sinners** lend to **sinners**, expecting to be repaid in full. (Luke 6:32–34 NIV, emphasis added)

> For just as through the disobedience of the one man the many were made **sinners,** so also through the obedience of the one man the many will be made righteous. (Rom. 5:19 NIV, emphasis added)

These passages (along with many others we don't have enough space to consider in this book) show us that the title of "sinner" is most often used in Scripture not when identifying Christians but when identifying those who don't know Jesus yet. There are a couple exceptions, but if you investigate for yourself (and you should!), you'll find in the vast majority of cases, the term "sinner" just isn't the way the New Testament writers choose to refer to believers.

Again, hear me out: I'm not saying sin's presence is gone or that it is something we will never wrestle with in this life. Certainly not! Rather, I'm saying that though the *presence* of sin remains, it has lost its *power* to define who we are in the eyes of God because what He sees is the righteousness of Christ, which covers us completely. I'm saying that, in Scripture, a person with a saving faith in Jesus Christ is almost never *identified* as a sinner, which leads us to believe we shouldn't claim this as our primary identity, either. It's worth considering that we might even be disrespecting the new identities granted us when we refuse to accept our new names.

putting off the old self

Does this mean we have lost our ability to sin? By no means. Of course we can still sin, and given the strength of our flesh, we are in constant need of confession and repentance.

More than one hundred verses mention our propensity to sin. Because of this, we must take sin seriously like the Bible does. And in the New Testament books of Colossians, Ephesians, Romans, Galatians, 1 Peter, 1 John, Hebrews, and 1 Timothy, we are told exactly how to do that—by **putting off** the old self and then **putting on** our new identities in Christ.

Paul says it this way in Ephesians 4:22, 24: "Lay aside the old self, . . . and put on the new self, which in the likeness of God has been created in righteousness and holiness of the truth" (NASB1995).

While we are learning that we are not *identified* as sinners after we have received salvation from Jesus, we can never forget that on this side of heaven we will always battle with sin. We must take sin seriously, fight it wisely, and put it off in the power of the Holy Spirit. By naming our sin, confessing it, fighting it, and stubbornly choosing to walk in victory over it, we learn how to walk in our identity as "saints."

Our change isn't completely unlike the caterpillar's journey in becoming a butterfly.[28] It doesn't matter how much a caterpillar might try to ascend into the air; it just can't. There aren't a few self-help strategies that can fix its inabilities. Its legs and furry skin can't just be improved. It needs to be transformed into an entirely *new creation* if it's going to operate in the sky instead of on land. And miraculously, God provides an incredible metamorphosis that enables us to see that He, in fact, is able to make one thing into something entirely different. After a period, a caterpillar becomes a completely new creature, fit for new purposes.

But here's the catch: this new creature is still a part of the same world, but now it has to learn to fly. This creature had spent its *entire lifetime* before this moment operating as a crawling insect. It will take time to operate as a new creature. After its time in the chrysalis, it hangs upside down from it for some time. Its wings must dry and expand. They must harden to give the butterfly the form that will enable it to fly.

I imagine that the first moments of flight for a new butterfly feel rather jerky and odd. It probably takes some time to get into a good rhythm. The flapping probably feels wobbly at first.

Does this wobbling mean the butterfly is not a new creation after all? No. It means that it had spent most of its life in nature ingrained in old ways, and it will take time in this new life to operate in new ones. But all the while, *it's still obviously a new creation*. It just takes a bit of time to know how to live like it.

And so it goes for you and me when it comes to sin. We lived as one type of creature for years, and we were accustomed to old ways. But our Father made us new creations. The same world is all around us—it's not gone. But we are now identified as citizens of a new kingdom.

Plain as day, before the living God, we're new creations. But it takes time to learn how to put off the old ways—to let the old, deeply engrained habits die—and put on the new. We will have difficult days. We can still operate as our former selves, forgetting we're not who we once were anymore. Our old habits call to us.

And yet we are still new creations. We're just learning how to fly. This is what it means to be a once-sinner saved by grace, learning how to walk as a saint.

Indeed, the identity of sinner exists in Scripture—we cannot deny that or brush it off as if it's not a big deal. But it is an identity we learn to *put off* in favor of *putting on* the identity of saint.

the saint in Scripture

It's not a word all of us use in our church circles.

Yet, when we look at the history of the broader church, there is a rich heritage of honoring our brothers and sisters in the faith as saints. The writer of Hebrews 12:1 encourages us to remember that we are not running this race alone; rather we are "surrounded by such a great cloud of witnesses" (NIV), the saints who have gone before us.

When you think of people who are "saints," whose faces come to mind? It's possible that you think of someone who is "extra" holy or someone who has achieved a specific status in the community of faith. Maybe a select few names come to your mind . . . Saint Peter,

Saint Thomas Aquinas, Saint Patrick, or Saint Teresa . . . and you think, *I could never be like those people.*

On the other hand, the face coming to mind might be Aunt Susie—you know, the one who everyone says is "just a saint" for volunteering to wash the dishes by hand every Christmas.

The more we read the Scriptures, the more the word *saint* becomes familiar, as it is used more than sixty times in the New Testament. The word *saint* literally means "set apart" and "holy."[29]

But here is the catch: in the New Testament, the word is used to refer to *all* those who follow Jesus, not just some select few!

Don't take my word for it. Look at these verses!

> For through him we both have access in one Spirit to the Father. So, then, you are no longer foreigners and strangers, **but fellow citizens with the saints**, and members of God's household, built on the foundation of the apostles and prophets, with Christ Jesus himself as the cornerstone. (Eph 2:18–20, emphasis added)

> To the church of God at Corinth, to those sanctified in Christ Jesus, **called as saints**, with all those in every place who call on the name of Jesus Christ our Lord—both their Lord and ours. (1 Cor 1:2, emphasis added)

> . . . joyfully giving thanks to the Father, who has enabled you to **share in the saints' inheritance in the light**. He has rescued us from the domain of darkness and transferred us into the kingdom of the Son he loves. (Col. 1:11–13, emphasis added)

> Paul and Timothy, servants of Christ Jesus: *To all the*
> *saints in Christ Jesus* who are in Philippi....For we are
> the circumcision, the ones who worship by the Spirit of
> God, boast in Christ Jesus, and do not put confidence in
> the flesh. (Phil. 1:1; 3:3, emphasis added)

> To all who are in Rome, loved by God, *called as saints*.
> Grace to you and peace from God our Father and the
> Lord Jesus Christ...I thank my God through Jesus
> Christ for all of you because the news of your faith is
> being reported in all the world. (Rom. 1:7–8, emphasis
> added)

The assumption was that those men and women who followed Christ had received a righteousness that was not their own doing but was theirs by grace and through faith in Christ. Because of Christ and through the power of the Holy Spirit, God's people are now able to live "set apart" and "holy" lives that not only worship Him but also bless the world. You could say they are *saints saved by grace*. They could never have achieved this title on their own. It required His mercy and grace because they were sinners . . . and they still sinned. But it was a new day.

Can you take it in—the glory of it all?

Jesus had come, and with His invitation He had new identities to distribute to all those who would follow Him wholeheartedly, and Paul addresses them as such. And not just a select few. Notice how far-reaching these verses go in terms of geography and audience. Corinthians. Ephesians. Colossians. Philippians. Romans. The list could go on. It doesn't matter which letter Paul is writing to believers, or in which city they reside, Paul calls them all saints! If they are in Christ, he is sure—they have a new identity, and that identity is "saint." The same goes for you and for me.

embracing identity

Sometimes we forget the glory of the fact that we have this new identity from Jesus. It might be possible to recapture the wonder of it all as you read this story from an orphanage for the deaf and blind in China.

China is a country that once had a one-child limit—a country where, historically speaking, weaker children haven't had many chances to succeed. The world around them hasn't typically emphasized the value of these kids, so they are surprised when they hear otherwise.

In 2013, Chinese missionary John Bentley described a moment when they were given a translation of a book by Max Lucado called *You Are Special*, a book that I (Kathryn) have often read to my own kids.

The story describes Punchinello, a wooden person in a village of wooden people. The villagers had a practice of sticking stars on the achievers and dots on the strugglers.

Punchinello had so many dots that people gave him more dots for no reason at all. But then he met Eli, his maker. Eli affirmed him, telling him to disregard the opinion of others. "I made you," he explained. "I don't make mistakes." Punchinello had never heard such words. When he did, his dots began to fall off. And when the children in the Chinese orphanage heard such words, their worlds began to change.

Bentley said:

> When they first distributed these books to the children
> and staff of the deaf school, the most bizarre thing
> happened. At a certain point everyone started crying. I
> could not understand this reaction. . . . Americans are

somewhat used to the idea of positive reinforcement....
Not so in China and particularly not for these children
who are virtually abandoned and considered valueless
by their natural parents because they were born "broken." When the idea came through in the reading that
they are special simply because they were made by a
loving Creator ... everyone started crying—including
their teachers! It was wild.[30]

But on some level, we relate. Many of us feel our "dots" and try to
get rid of them unsuccessfully.

Maybe sometimes we need to remember our identity first, to go
back to our Maker and all that He has said about us. We will always
have dots—our sins and struggles—but this doesn't define us.
Sometimes it takes embracing our identity by our Maker for the
dots to begin falling off.

who we really are

Our battle with sin and our own limitations will never cease to be
a reality during our time on earth. We fight with it to respect this
holy identity we've been given. This process of dealing with our sin,
with God's help, while reminding ourselves of our given identity, is
a lifelong duality we must step into.

We are, as Martin Luther famously says, "*Simul Justus et Peccator.*" At
the same time justified and still sinners. I don't think the apostle
Paul would disagree with Luther on that, but in terms of how often
he uses one identifier over the other in the New Testament, Paul is
clearly stuck on *primarily* referring to believers as "saints," literally
"holy ones," in all his letters. While not dismissing our propensity
to sin, he wants Christians to identify themselves in regard to
their new natures, not their old. Who they really are is saints who
fight against sin, not sinners who sometimes get it right. This

acknowledgment of our identity can have great repercussions on the way we live our lives.

Consider how Michael Kruger puts it:

> When our true identities are understood rightly, it actually affects the way we view our sins. We might think that the best way to appreciate the depth of our sin is to think of ourselves primarily in the category of "sinners." But this can actually have the opposite effect.[31]

How so, you might wonder? Kruger goes on:

> If we think of ourselves only as "sinners" then our sins are seen as something rather ordinary and inevitable. They are just the result of who we are. Sure, we wish we didn't sin. But, that's just what "sinners" do.[32]

And then he brings the better alternative:

> If we instead view ourselves as "saints," then we will begin to see our sin in a whole new light. If we really are "holy ones," then whatever sins we commit are a deeper, more profound, and more serious departure from God's calling than we ever realized. Our sin, in a sense, is even more heinous because it is being done by those who now have new natures and a new identity. And it is this "cognitive dissonance" between our identities as saints and our sinful actions that leads us to repentance. We repent because these sins are *not* ordinary and expected. They are fundamentally contrary to who God has made us to be. It is this tension between our identities and our actions that is lost when we cease to think of ourselves as saints.[33]

In other words, when we actually dare to *receive* the new name God has given us, we can begin to embody the actions and hearts associated with that name. It is true that we can sin, but what is *most* true about us is that we are saints in Christ.

This is **who we are**.

cellist of sarajevo

In 1992, the city of Sarajevo, the capital of Bosnia and Herzegovina, came under siege during the Bosnian War. The siege of Sarajevo was terribly violent and became known as the longest siege of a capital city in the history of modern warfare. Over many months, combinations of mortar bombings, artillery attacks, and small arms battles left the city standing in its own rubble and living in ongoing fear and panic. Shortly after one such attack that devastated a town square and killed twenty-two people innocently waiting in line to receive food, cellist Vedran Smailovic did the unthinkable.

Dressed in his finely chosen performance attire, he calmly walked through the rubble of the town square and sat down among the ruins and began to play his cello. Under the threat of snipers, at the risk of his own life, his melodies echoed throughout the streets of Sarajevo. His courageous presence and the beauty of his music stood in contrast to the violence and devastation overtaking the city.

This story reminds us of the greatest story being told.

Similar to the city of Sarajevo, our cities lie in ruins. We have all contributed to the chaos and calamity. We recognize the world isn't as it should be, we are not as we should be, and we long for healing and restoration. Apart from the Redeemer, we would be left alone, broken and wandering through life without hope. Yet Jesus, robed in human flesh, comes to sit with us. Amid the rubble, He plays a different melody. Risking His own life, and ultimately laying it down on our behalf, He makes a way for us both to recover what was lost and to find freedom from sin's enslaving power. Jesus, the perfect image of the Father, makes a way for His image to be restored in us. Jesus, the perfect sinless man, makes a way for us to find freedom from the bondage of sin.

We find ourselves now living in a city that is no longer defined by its ruins and among a people who are no longer defined by their ruinous actions. Somehow, only through extreme grace, we are now rebuilders in a kingdom that never ends. We now labor alongside a King who is known for recreating and restoring. And being such, we are a "city set on a hill," as Jesus says, that shines a light and points a world in ruin to a better story, a sweeter song, and a living picture of beauty.

moving forward together

What could it mean for us as we walk ahead, aware of our sin, but in awareness of our new identities? What should we expect if we embrace the new while fighting off the old?

first, we should expect it to cultivate humility in us

Because we are forever confronted with sin, we will always be intimately acquainted with our need for Christ. Our growing awareness of our new identity won't make us proud; it will actually bear the fruit of humility in our lives as we seek to fight off the old ways that work against it.

second, we should expect to walk in greater confidence

When we accept our new name, we accept everything that name brings with it. When we know we are saints of the Most High, we can approach God with confidence, and because of that, we can stand firm in who we are because our lives have been hidden with Christ, and He now lives within us.

your whole identity

With your whole life before you, let's look at how you can grow into all of who God says you are.

consider this if you need to grow in confession and repentance over sin

Could one or more of these help expand the way you relate to God?

- In your prayer time, make a habit to include a time of confession, reflecting on your actions and sin in your heart over the past day or week.
- Ask God to remind you of the price of His sacrifice on the cross for us all.
- Find a relationship where you can openly confess your struggles and ask for prayer.
- Create a list of old habits that are particularly hard to "put off" for you. Consider what current practices in your life might be granting room for these habits to stick around. Lastly, come up with some ways you might give these practices less room to grow.

consider this, if you need to grow into your new identity as a saint

Could these expand the way you relate to God?

- Write out the names Jesus calls us as believers, and display them somewhere so you can see them daily.

- Thank God in your prayer times that we aren't defined by our past and that He has supernaturally given us, as believers, a new heart and a new name.

- Ask God to move you into a season of embracing the power of walking in your new identity with joy.

- Make a list of what the New Testament says about the old self and the new self (see Gal. 5:19–21; Col. 3:5–17; Eph. 4:20–5:5; 1 Cor. 3:3 for help). Think through some creative ways you can start walking in the things that are on the "new self" list.

for seekers and sleepers

Before we conclude this book, we wanted to address those of you whose hearts are longing for a foundational assurance about your faith before you can move forward with the things written to followers of Jesus in these pages.

- Some of you found yourself here because someone invited you to read this book, or you picked it up on a whim. Thankfully you have made it to this point. Though you don't consider yourself a follower of Jesus, you are seeking something greater spiritually, and maybe as you've read this book, you sense that Jesus might be calling you to Himself. You are open to what it means to follow Jesus with your life.

- Others of you have been in the church for a time, but you've been asleep in your faith. You've been going through the motions and playing the part, but your life doesn't reflect much of Jesus's life. Maybe something in the

words you have read here has fanned a flame
in your heart for something more than what
you've been experiencing. Your old faith needs
a new power.

If you are in either of these situations, the invitation of Jesus, some
of which you have seen on the pages of this book, is extended to
you. If your heart is sensing that there is more abundance of life
ahead for you, your heart is right. Maybe you need to hear and
respond to Jesus's offer:

"Come, follow me." (Matt. 4:19 NIV)

Your life will never be the same.

conclusion // whole

Inhale.

       Exhale.

Inhale.

       Exhale.

Oh, the satisfaction it brings to just complete the breathing cycle. The inhale and the exhale. Only when we complete them both do we fully take advantage of God's design for the functioning of our lungs and our bodies.

After reading the four sections of this book, perhaps you have found that you've personally chosen to be, in essence, a chronic inhaler in certain areas of your spirituality. Or maybe you're a person on the flip side—a chronic exhaler. You have settled for half when God has invited you to be whole. Hopefully by now you have identified the ways you can begin to step into fullness of life with God in areas where you have settled for less.

What could it look like to move forward, engaging all of God:

       with your head *and* your heart?

       in truth *and* in spirit?

in your being *and* in your doing?

in the reality of being both a sinner *and* a saint?

It looks like vitality. It looks like a more well-rounded view of life with God than you've ever experienced. It looks more like an intimate and dynamic relationship with the One who created you in fullness from the beginning.

As we have mentioned, you will hear some people call for balance.

Let's inhale, and let's exhale, but let's do it with a moderate amount of our lungs' capacity. Let's make sure our inhale never exceeds or overshadows our exhale, or vice versa.

This is like aiming for shallow breathing. *Or breathing minimally instead of deeply.*

This defies the invitation to abundance of life! It silences the opportunity to a life-giving, full-lung-capacity inhale and exhale. While balance can be a noble aspiration in some areas of our lives, when it comes to our relationship with God, we are invited to go "all in" in every area!

God wants us to love Him with *all* of our head and all of our heart.

He calls us to worship Him *in the fullness* of Spirit and truth.

He wants us to abide in Him *so deeply* that our being and doing produce more fruit than we have ever seen in our lives.

He desires for us to step *increasingly* into our new identities so that we may become *who we really are* in Christ.

He invites us to be *whole*.

The invitation is ours. The question that remains is this: *Will you and I step into wholeness, or will we continue to live segmented lives?* If you are like us, there is really no question at all; we are hungry for all that God has for us, for the glory of His name. Irenaeus, a second-century Greek bishop, once said, "The glory of God is a human being fully alive."[34] So let us step into fullness of life with God so that we may become fully alive, bearing His glory in the world every single day.

We leave you with this simple prayer:

God,
You are here.
You've always been fully here,
bringing all that You are to me.
And now, finally,
in return,
I am fully here with You.
Help me relate to You
with all that I am.

notes

1. Sam Storms, *Practicing the Power: Welcoming the Gifts of the Holy Spirit in Your Life* (Grand Rapids: Zondervan, 2017), 219.
2. Storms, *Practicing the Power*, 220.
3. "Barna: State of the Church," February, 19, 2020, https://www.barna.com/research/current-perceptions.
4. "Barna: State of the Church."
5. "Lev/Heart," Bible Project, The Shema Series, accessed April 30, 2022, www.thebibleproject.com/explore/video/lev-heart.
6. Andrew Wilson, *Unbreakable: What the Son of God Said about the Word of God* (Leyland, Lancashire, England: 10Publishing, 2014), 507.
7. Goleman and Dalai Lama, "Nature Communications," Department of Psychology at Queen's University in Canada, 2020, *Harvard Business Review*, 2004.
8. James K. A. Smith, *You Are What You Love: The Spiritual Power of Habit* (Grand Rapids: Brazos Press, 2016), 1.
9. Wilson, *Unbreakable*, 507.
10. Storms, *Practicing the Power*, 220.
11. Storms, *Practicing the Power*, 220.
12. Storms, *Practicing the Power*, 24.
13. J. D. Greear, "Be Filled with the Spirit," accessed May 3, 2022, https://summitchurch.com/GetFile.ashx?Guid=aace5ede-81de-4e1d-95bd-f26809bd21b4.
14. This paragraph is informed by Andrew Marin, "Here Are the Old Testament Scripture References that Jesus Quoted More Than Anything Else," Patheos, November 16, 2010, https://www.patheos.com/blogs/loveisanorientation/2010/11/here-are-the-old-testament-scripture-references-that-jesus-quoted-more-than-anything-else.
15. George Müller, Susannah Grace Sanger Müller, Arthur T. Pierson, *God Had Mercy on Me: The Life and Work of George Müller* (Stuttgart, Germany: e-artnow, 2020), 19.
16. "Mens," PLUS, accessed May 5, 2022, https://www.biblestudytools.com/lexicons/greek/kjv/meno.html.
17. Adam Wernick and Annie Minoff, "A new study found people are terrible at sitting alone with their thoughts. How about you?" *Science Friday, The World*, July 19, 2014, https://theworld.org/stories/2014-07-19/new-study-found-people-are-terrible-sitting-alone-their-thoughts-how-about-you.
18. Blaise Pascal, *Pensees*, 1654.
19. This phrase is coined by Apple executive Linda Stone; https://thesystemsthinker.com/continuous-partial-attention-and-the-demise-of-discretionary-time/.
20. Eugene H. Peterson, *Subversive Spirituality* (Grand Rapids: Eerdmans, 1997), 14.
21. Barry Jones, *Dwell with God for the World* (Downers Grove, IL: IVP Books, 2014).

WHOLE

22. Jen Pollock Michel, "Salt and Light in a World of Decay and Darkness," in Hannah Anderson, Jada Edwards, Jasmine L. Holmes, et al., *World on Fire: Walking in the Wisdom of Christ When Everyone's Fighting about Everything* (Nashville: B&H, 2021), 136.

23. Michel, "Salt and Light," 134.

24. Peterson, *Subversive Spirituality*, 14.

25. George Müller, Susannah Grace Sanger Müller, Arthur T. Pierson, *God Had Mercy on Me: The Life and Work of George Müller* (Stuttgart, Germany: e-artnow, 2020), 93.

26. Müller and Sanger Müller, et al, *God Had Mercy on Me*, 74.

27. Müller and Sanger Müller, et al, *God Had Mercy on Me*, 402.

28. The information in this paragraph is provided by "How Do Butterflies/Moths Spread Their Wings after Emerging?", Reiman Gardens, Iowa State University, accessed May 9, 2022, https://www.reimangardens.com/butterfly/butterfliesmoths-spread-wings-emerging.

29. "Comparing the Use of 'Christian' and 'Saint' in Scriptures," Deseret News, April 22, 2012, https://www.deseret.com/2012/4/22/20501425/comparing-the-use-of-christian-and-saint-in-scriptures?_amp=true.

30. "You Are Special," Jentezen Franklin, March 16, 2013, https://jentezenfranklin.org/daily-devotions/you-are-special.

31. Michael Kruger, on the Canon Fodder blog, here: https://www.michaeljkruger.com/saint-or-sinner-rethinking-the-language-of-our-christian-identity/.

32. Michael Kruger, on the Canon Fodder blog, here: https://www.michaeljkruger.com/saint-or-sinner-rethinking-the-language-of-our-christian-identity/.

33. Michael Kruger, on the Canon Fodder blog, here: https://www.michaeljkruger.com/saint-or-sinner-rethinking-the-language-of-our-christian-identity/.

34. James R. Payton, *Irenaeus on the Christian Faith: A Condensation of Against Heresies* (Pickwick Publications, 2011), 116.